Possibility Thinking: Explorations in Logic and Thought
by Justin Coslor

This book has many errors in it so please remember to be kind to
everyone and only read it gently when you are in a good mood and if you
get tired then gently stop and do something else such as sleep and dream
of peace. The diagrams and drawings and stuff for that book are in the
difficult to follow though sometimes interesting for me to think about
and they are not perfect either so please be kind and try not to treat
anyone badly, and please do not treat me badly. Thank you. More formal
thought about that could perhaps be carefully edited by hand.
PICForm Compiler Project
Perhaps people could make a program that makes writing C programs
easier. I think that C stands for subset.
It could be a program that translates PICFORM
cross-domain relations into C programs and data structures.
Computation: COMPUTATION IS A MEANS OF SOLVING PROBLEMS. IT IS
APPLIED STRATEGY, AS AN APPLICATION OF NUMERICAL DIMENSIONS TO
QUALITATIVE ASPECTS OF A MENTAL MODEL, SO THAT PATTERNS ARE ABLE TO BE
IDENTIFIED AND CONTEXTUALIZED COMPUTABLY BY PEOPLE. I have noticed that
wide sweeping statements and humor do not translate very well.

One of the ways to invent stuff.
Make a system to list topics next to each other
with a selection of topics to find some useful compatibilities
of their relations. It requires helpful compassionate
human beings and a beautiful diversity of other life as
all life can be beautiful if nurtured to be compassionate.
Helpful thinkers with many skills are needed to think about the topics
in the discovery of new ideas and new profound concepts and
considerations. Concepts are contextual perceptions. A continuum of
textuality is like the setting in a story and is what a context
is. Often it is said that a picture, such as a drawing or diagram, is
worth a thousand words. Sometimes less is more with words. It
sometimes helps to simplify and it sometimes helps to elaborate. It
helps to try to do a good job and plan ahead and leave plenty
for the future.

Summary of some ideas from Possibility Thinking ::
Sine Spiral Graphing note: many waveforms are perpendicular side views of
spirals and complex spirals. The Unit Circle is a front view of a spiral
or complex spiral.
If data has recognizable features then it is a pattern.

Repetition is what makes a symmetry and is what makes a patterns'
features recognizable to some.
Information is a symphony of symbolism and symmetry.
Information, by it's very nature is a division.
Yet it strives to become whole again, and at the very least,
to become balanced.
All truth is but an approximation of a deeper truth.
What the world needs more of in order to support the population
is more industries. An entire industry can be created simply by
making a new kind of algorithm, such as a new adjective.
Perhaps an algorithm that creates a helpful niche for people to fill or
make use of via services or products.
An algorithm can be developed by applying an axiom to a new context.
Contexts are composed of networks of patterns,
patterns are composed of networks of variables,
and variables are composed of networks of properties
(first principle dimensions such as adjectives).
In considering ideas and information that is new to me,
I ask networks of questions.
The questions can be framed as dependency charts.
Now what is a good way to understand dependency charts?
List out the major nodes (most well-connected nodes)
as open-ended definitions and form lexicons out of the interconnected
definitions. Next, map out the rest of the nodes axiomatically using
those definition structures. Turn this into a software for common sense
perception. Maybe make a free cognition engine that can learn the
meaning behind things so that it can solve problems by figuring out new
ways of thinking about things such as by adapting the context of
question
/perception networks or another helpful way.
What metric makes an analogy recognizable?
KNOWLEDGE MINUS WISDOM EQUALS NOTHING
Thoughtforms are to Metaphor as Plurality is to Interconnectivity.
Thoughtforms : Metaphor :: Plurality : Interconnectivity
: = Thoughtforms
:: = Metaphor
Form networks of questions to gain valuable perspectives on
topical and problem data. Model question engines in a careful
goal manner with sustainability and capability and filling necessity as
the primary objectives.
Example: Make a question network. Draw a picture.
....
  .
  .
  .
  .
  .
  .
  .
  .
  .
  .
  .
....
Basic question thoughtforms:
Why? = Is there a reason for how this came to be, and what is it?
What? = The existance of this shall be called by a name that needs to

be defined, and we are inquiring about that.
When? = This occurred or shall occur at what time and day?
How? = By what process does this function?
Notice that I had to use "what" in every one of these...
Except I tried not to use "what" in it's own definition, which was
difficult.
"That" = a pointer to a specific instance of something in existence...
Whether it be in physical or virtual reality.
The difference between virtual objects and physical objects is that
virtual objects are just pointers to other pointers.
Physical objects are pointers that point to themselves in a loop
of circular reasoning. To loop is to group. A dot can loop a line.
Sometimes experimentation is necessary to solve problems and to answer
questions because some nodes of information or questions or contextual
perception networks are otherwise unreachable, and often entirely unknown
to exist. We are surrounded by answers. However, if they are meaningless
and often impossible to detect without knowing at least some of the
questions that they are derived from, then without a question/answer
connection, the consciousness of awareness may not exist as well it may.

Please remember to not treat anyone badly.
observe
.
The Certainty Principle
    When anyone observes someone they
change them and the observer is always
also changed by that which they observe.
So worry not about that which is temporary
and instead think long and deeply about
how to treat everyone well as that is the
proof by example that lasts forever.
.
Accuracy
.
Symmetry + Precision -> Accuracy -> Efficiency
Accuracy -> Clear Thinking -> Logical Reasoning
Logical Reasoning -> Organization
Organization -> Tool Adaptability -> Resource Management
Resource Management -> Sustainability -> Repeatability
Sustainability -> Reliability -> Freedom
Repeatability -> Mobility -> Liberty
Honesty -> Trust -> Diplomacy -> Symbiosis -> Justice
Freedom + Liberty + Justice -> Virtue
Virtue -> Harmony Without Harm -> Friendly Intelligence
Tool Adaptability -> Creativity
Honesty + Love + Logic -> Wisdom
.
Nurture Thought
We all know a lot more than
we even know. We do not know
what we can know and we do not know
what we can not know. We do forget.
We do not know something until
we know it and then we know it.
Then it becomes out of sight and
out of mind as a baby seed of
potential that can grow if nurtured.

.
Suffixes
The suffix er is erronious.
The suffix est is especially temporary.
.
Juxtapositions
is is In Synchronous
equals is = therefore 1 = 1 AND 0 = 0
YES = YES
NO = NO
+ = plus = YES AND YES
- = minus = NO AND NO
therefore = .:
: = analogy = is to = are to
:: = metaphor = as
.
KNOWLEDGE MINUS WISDOM EQUALS NOTHING
Thoughtforms : Metaphor :: Plurality : Interconnectivity
Thoughtforms are to Metmetaphor as Plurality is to Interconnectivity.
Thoughtform is to Metaphor as Oneness is to Interconnectivity.
Oneness = Mono = Monality
We are of a common seed long ago.
Words are semantics and symbols are syntax.
Words + Symbols = Knowledge
Wisdom comes from Oneness and Knowledge is translated Wisdom in Plurality.
Knowledge is a gateway to Wisdom.
Intention is the ion of intent.
Priority is before reality.
Priority is a principle ion of reality.
is = in synchronous
Ion is a gateway of dimension as a thought in a dot.
A dot can loop a line. To loop is to group.
Knowledge as patterns in contexts.
Thinking as storing and grouping knowledge.
Grouping is a way of networking knowledge.
Intention is the inverse of tension before reality, as a free flowing ion.
Metaphor analyzes the logic of thoughtforms plurality of
interconnectivity.
Knowledge -> Wisdom
Knowledge leads to Wisdom.
KNOWLEDGE - WISDOM =
KNOWLEDGE MINUS WISDOM LEADS TO NOTHING
? = QUESTION = QUEST ION = QUALITY UNION ESPECIALLY TEMPORARY ION.
Something like that or something.
.

Explorations in Logic and Thought ::
Even though we forget, we just do the best that we know how in each moment.

If you would like to donate then read this page:
If you want to donate something I only accept Post Office Money Orders.
Please be kind to everyone. Thank you.

JUSTIN M COSLOR
PO BOX 367
MOUNT VERNON, WA

98273

.

Possibility Thinking:
Explorations in Logic and Thought
by Justin Coslor

Possibility Thinking:
Explorations in Logic and Thought
by Justin Coslor
                        ****
                        Table of Contents:
                        ****

                              Book I:
                        Patterns In Contexts

Book II:
Networks of Questions

Book III:
Math Ideas:

```
                      ----------------------
                             Book V:
                        Philosophy & Quotes
                      ----------------------
```

```
-------------------------------------------------------------
-------------------------------------------------------------
-------------------------------------------------------------
```
The following Dates and Copyrights and Names and Titles do not matter.
```
-------------------------------------------------------------
-------------------------------------------------------------
-------------------------------------------------------------
-------------------------------------------------------------
```

```
                      ----------------------
                             Book I:
                        Patterns In Contexts
```

Stuff that occurred to me while going through some of my old journal entries
(about eight pages worth).

Analogies mimic patterns across contexts via cross-domain relations.
That's the basis of Analogical Reasoning. Every pattern in every context
is unique to the properties and axioms of the contexts they exist in.

I've written this book without doing a lick of research or reading
(except where indicated on a few entries), as an experiment to see if I
could generate some new foundations of knowledge and understanding. Some
experts say I succeeded.

A symmetry is an example of an internal algebra. Unique symmetries are
atomic repetitions, and are the simplest form of patterns, distinct from
perceptually apparently random chaos. (I don't believe in ultimate
randomness).

Analogical mimicing results in similar, yet distinctly different patterns.
All truth is but an approximation of a deeper truth. Understanding is
subject to computational complexity of the perceiver and the data forms and
content perceived.

Knowledge is the quest of discovery, and understanding is the growth of
the perceiver. It's how possibilities happen through careful navigation.
There are no dead ends.

Mark fundamental landmark differences in analogically mimiced patterns,
for possible classification category augmentations (for navigation and
data retrieval purposes). Beware of oversimplification of data streams
in order to fit a pattern into a perceptual mold.

Even if my ideas overlap with existing knowledge, they provide a new way
of understanding that knowledge, and that is valuable because my ideas
are not based on mimicry since I haven't studied topics related to them
much (except a college philosophy course and K-13 math). These ideas
exist for the most part in their own context. They can be no doubt eventually
be linked to ideas in other contexts though. Lexicons can often be linked to
external contexts.

Numbers & Patterns Across Contexts

Metaphorically speaking, prime numbers are injective and composite numbers
are surjective, when translating functions from one context to another.
Similarly, single-repetition patterns are injective and composite
patterns are surjective, when translating relations from one context to
another. This is an essential part of analogical reasoning.

Property grouping axioms in cross-domain relations.
(See diagram.)
1. All variables have properties.
2. All properties are independent of their variable's context(s).
3. All properties have some combination of qualitative relations,
quantitative relations, existential locations, and existential
conditions.
4. Every variable exists within a context and can vary
from context to context.
5. Contexts are composed of networks of patterns, patterns are composed of
networks of variables, and variables are composed of networks of properties.
6. Information can be represented as patterns in contexts, and in that way it
can be represented metaphorically through analogical reasoning and
abdicative reasoning. Relations of various kinds, location(s), and
condition(s) (apon and of) exist at all of the various levels, and those
are the data access points.

Properties
These are first-level definitions of some useful kinds of properties, any of
which can be networked together to create relations and variables and
patterns and contexts that may exist in physical and/or platonic reality:
----
* qualitative identifiers: Categorical names and cross-references.
* qualitative factors: Qualitative pieces of composite patterns.
* quantitative identifiers: Cardinalities (orderings), scalers, and surjective
equalities.
* quantitative factors: Representational methods of measurement of dimension
sets.
* states: Observable distinct configurations that mark and increment step
counts.
* conditions: Dependencies that distinctly configure each state.
* cycle counts: A tally that is increased with each repetition of a process.
* recursions: A self-defined process or network (an internal algebra), or a
function that calls itself.
* repetitions: An algebra, atomic elements that repeat, composite patterns
that repeat, or symmetries.
* activity level: The number of cycles per step (positive, negative, random,
or null).
* step counts: A tally that is increased as conditions of each state
transition is reached.
* location: A place in a memory grid where identifiable data is stored.
* positions: The sequence coordinates of variable in N-dimensional orderings.
* orientations: The perspective that data maps are observed from: This may be
contextual, or spatially framed position maps, and perspectives may even
have translation conditions of their own.

As you can see, activity level is just one kind of property, and priority
systems such as neural nets can be based on that property. Other kinds
of systems can be based on other properties.
----
* Relations are the juxtaposition of infrastructures, which result in an
output.

Patterns In Contexts: Neural Nets As Priority Systems
    Neural nets are essentially priority systems for allocating and
de-allocating priorities of networked elements such as variables on a grid.
Each network can be considered a context, and can be said to be a network of
patterns composed of variables and relations. If the patterns are
functions, then the priority of each pattern determines the level of activity
(cycles per step) of each pattern's function(s).
    Some priority level results in a random level of activity, and the other
priority levels result in either positive levels of activity, negative
(reverse) levels of activity, and an undefined priority setting results
in no activity.
    Example:
Context: ABCDEFG * R1R2R3R4R5R6R7R8 == a network of patterns (see diagram).
Where each pattern == (a variable)(a relation Rn), and the level of activity
of each pattern is:
(undefined, -3, -2, -1, random, 1, 2. 3)(a variable)(a relation Rn),
and the activity level determines how many cycles per step that the
relation Rn operates on the variable, and the pattern it is linked
to. These values could be anything, this is just an example.
    Activity level is one type of property of the variable.

***Variables are composed of networks of properties.
***Patterns are composed of networks of variables and relations.
***Contexts are composed of networks of patterns and relations to other
contexts. Properties can be things like qualitative and quantitative
identifiers and factors, states, conditions, cycle counts, recursions
and repetitions, activity level (cycles per step), step counts, locations,
positions, orientations, etc.
Patterns in Contexts:
a computational model for representing information metaphorically
through abdicative reasoning.
All ideas herein are Copyright by Justin Coslor on their respective dates.
These notes are a progression of the concepts in the order they occured to me.
This occured to me as a pseudo-sophomore at Carnegie Mellon University in
Pittsburgh, PA.
(It's a first draft so please forgive it's sketchyness.)
All knowledge=information, which can be represented as metaphors. Metaphors
are applied to specific contexts and contexts=multiple contexts.
A. All knowledge is metaphors applied to >= 1 context.
B. A metaphor is a set of associations (links, patterns) that can or is
applied to a context.
A single context...A single specific context...general/nonspecific contexts.
C. A context is a set of restrictions (restrictions on information,
associations, links, patterns, sometimes even contexts).
Therefore the statement A is equivalent to this statement:
"Each piece of knowledge is a set of associations that can be applied to >= 1
set(s) of restrictions."

The use of this I had in mind is to make a computer software that could
understand and manipulate (and maybe even apply) metaphors. Many other ideas
occurred to me today too, possibly due to doing yogi breathing and meditation
exercises and taking vitamins since my health had been suffering.
Epistemology Framework for artificial intelligence "Patterns in
Contexts" continued...
----
* A pattern is a collection of symmetries, where each partition section of
data of every symmetry in the collection corresponds to another partition
section of data in that collection, or sometimes corresponds to a piece
or pieces of data in another collection (or other collections) which may or
may not be part of a similar symmetry in that other collection.
If data has recognizable features, it is a pattern. Repetition is what
makes a symmetry, and is what makes a pattern's features recognizable.
Unique partition sections of data are the atomic elements that a pattern's
features are composed of. A symmetry is a type of repetition,
but a repetition isn't always a symmetry (see metaphor definition below).
* A context is a map of patterns within (thus bounded by) either a set or
stream of data in which other patterns are ignored or are not apparent.
Or a context bounded by a larger pattern than the map itself
(which itself is a pattern that may or may not be part of the larger pattern),
such as the ordinal of the map or a pattern larger than the boundaries
of the scope. There can be many parallel streams, waves, or sets of data
in, traveling through, across, or around the self-updating mapping of
patterns which is chosen to be the context.
    Sometimes the corresponding partitions of data that make up a repetition
are translated by some pattern with each iteration, such as in a methaphor.
Yet similarity remains apparent (identifyable by some means).
Again, I believe that information is patterns in contexts, and that
information is metaphoric in nature. Tip: If confused by this write-up

of my premise, try reading the sentence in reverse order then back through
again.

Information is a symphony of symbolism and symmetry.
Information, by it's very nature, is a division. Yet it strives to become
whole again, and at the very least, to become balanced.

Category Theory: Abdicative context changing using identified
metaphoric patterns. Some dimension additions for alternating or specializing
the application of a pattern or set of patterns:
- Location
- Relative rate, relative timeline framework
- Newly recognized relations found under sequential and parallelly recursive
brute force and intuitively adaptive experimental logic search strategies --
Yields hypothetical considerations which can be temporally prioritized and
recursively checked and updated from state to state and organized
intelligently by current 1. depth, 2. branch size, 3. branch cardinality
(alpha-numeric, etc), 4. task growth rate, and 5. average task completion rate
(for scaling computability).

When you figure out why a variable is a variable in a particular way, that
understanding becomes a new relation to consider, which in effect and affect
either increases or decreases the dimensionality of the variable's context.
Some dimensions that are added usually increase task completion rate (such as
specialization) other dimensions that ar added usually increase task growth
rate (such as broadening the context or broadening the number of class
categories to consider). Generalization can in some cases merge categories,
classes, and/or contexts, or blur them for simplicity, and can increase or
decrease completion rate.

Generalization is useful for experimentation.
All truth is but an approximation of a deeper truth.
A pattern is like a function, and a context is like a field.
Each has relations, variables (when thought of metaphorically),
and often the potential for variations and unconsidered variables of
dimensionality.

A working definition of the mystery of consciousness might be ascribed to the
interplay between 1. perspective, 2. priorities, 3. intentions, and
4. awareness; all of which depend on the flexibility, state, and mechanisms of
belief held by the subject.

My data symmetry section analysis technique for perception through patterns in
contexts may be able to play a key role in automating axiom and theorem
discovery for any given context (i.e. contexts such as the integers, the
reals, wavefield analysis, map data, behavioral intention charts,
language/speech modeling and representation, transform sequences, etc.).
Any pattern discovered within a particular context can be applied to any of
the known axioms and theorems of that context, and patterns that are
discovered can sometimes be related to undiscovered axioms in that context.
Anytime an axiom or theorem is discovered in a context, the entire context is
redefined (as well as its subcontexts), and in doing so, its scope is
narrowed. Choose -> Search -> Experiment -> Classify -> Test -> Prove.
Choose/define context -> search for patterns -> searchfor patterns that relate
discovered patterns -> postulate a classification for each discovered
relation.
    For each relation, if a classification category does not exist that

closely matches the relation, then further experimentation, context choosing
(add and/or subtract context dimensions), and pattern searching must be done,
starting with the characteristics of all partially matched categories, until
an accurate or exact classification or category definition can be derived.
After the relation's category is realized, search for more examples of that
relation and derrive a proof of it. If the relation can be proven to be
applicable to all patterns in a given context and all subsets of that context,
it can be said to be an axiom of that context.

Context can be thought of as a network as well as a shell that encompasses
abstract nodes. The context of a set is merely its powerset, that is, until
relations are applied. I don't believe in randomness, but I do believe
that some contexts are larger or deeper than the scope of our perceptions.

A context can also be thought of as a network of patterns, or even the network
of relations that tlinks patterns. But when relations are applied to a
context, it becomes an organism. An organism that is capable of translation
(metaphoric operations), modification (adaptationn), division
(duplication/reproduction/partitioning, and/or growth and association with
other contexts.

There are patterns, and they exist within and between/across contexts, and
there are relations that act as reasoning engines that operate on the systems
of patterns and contexts.
    Patterns can have analogue distortion, digital distortion, or metaphoric
distortion. Contexts can be approximations of larger contexts, and
elaborations or extensions of smaller contets or extensions of other contexts
in general There can be relatively unique (somewhat unique, minimal
commonality) patterns and contexts. Note: the word "commonality" is based on
the greek root "monality", which is the "commonality" of the prime numbers.
Each prime number is a "co-monality." This can be visualized in terms of
geometry, to some extent. Every prime number is balanced, and is symmetrical,
and contains a unique number of dimensions, which are also unique kinds
of dimensions. Patterns and contexts and relations can also be symmetry pieces
of other patterns and contexts and relations, regardless of whether or not
they are distorted in any given state or piece or part or linkage.

Every context is founded on its own set of axioms and theorems, and adding an
axiom to or from a context's foundation fundamentally changes the context
profoundly, yet some structures may remain un-affected.
(*Note many of these notes may become invalid or ridiculous as you read more,
so mental filtering may be necessary.)

This is a quote from my journal.
    ""Metaphor" is a relational model of recursion, where the circular
reasoning (in recursive definitions & recursive functions) cross-relates
the elements of definitions & functions from multiple (or different)
contexts. That is why cross-domain relations are so crucial to the metaphoric
representation of knowledge and knowledge systems (logics)."

    "I also believe that information is metaphoric in nature (has algebraic
interconnectivity), and that it can be represented as a composition of
patterns in contexts, where the contexts themselves can be patterns, and the
atomic elements of each pattern are composed of symmetry sections
(partitiopns of data, where each partition is part of a local or dislocated
repetition (a symmetry, and algebra)). And it is only through the repetition
of a data section that part of a pattern can become recognizable from

apparently random white noise. Randomness and white noise are probably
patterns that are larger than the scope of our perceptions, so the data
appears random.

And I say that metaphors can be represented geometrically because all of
the prime numbers (the balance points in the universe) are symmetrical when
represented geometrically, and it is likely through primarily symmetrical
sensory and cognitive structures that our minds can interpret information.
And I think of metaphors not as A=B, but more like the similarity of the
juxtaposition of A's elements in the context of B, and B's elements in
the context of A, in terms of general systems theory.

I equate truth with workable patterns that become more and more refined
and defined as they get used. I believe that all truth that we are capable
of perceiving is but a small approximation of the whole truth. And that
the truth/patterns that we are capable of using is often subject to perception
within varying contexts. But there seem to exist connections between
information none-the-less, through whatever means. Possibly since (in my
opinion) everything came from oneness)."

Scope & Context -> Boundaries and Restrictions/Limitations
Class -> Purpose
Type -> Syntax
Pattern Definitions -> Semantics
Data Element Groups -> Configurations (Data Maps & Dependencies)

Patterns in Contexts Cognition Kernal
Database -> Metabase -> Context Rotator -> Experiment Application Field
Expandable
Adaptable
Translatable
Summarizable subjectively/objectively
======>
Metaphoric Linkers
Patterns Toolkit
Augmentation Socket Parameters
Analysis Scope Dimensionality
of (Input/Internal perspective "eyes")
Geometry & quantitative & qualitative properties of simultaneous interrupts
and their instantaneous functional interrelations and interactions
across multivariate sequence states (such as time & symmetry equivalencies).
*Every set state is but an approximation of the possible combinatorial
translations.
---------- Epistemology thoughts on Metaphor Abduction
Metaphors hide cross-domain relations between generalized nouns,
adjectives, and systems within a semi-subjective context of perspective.
The descriptive mappings of metaphors and multi-layered metaphoric operations
are generallymore foundational than their analogical counterparts, as the
metaphoric objects and relational context is generalized (from set, type, and
categorical specifics), which simplifies the computational complexity of the
models' qualitative factors, and provides new bases for consideration and
re-application of data, relations, and knowledge. Metaphor generation provides
the architectural basis and objective of considering newe relations and data
experimentatiopn for deriving and arriving at new models of understanding.
data --> context unknown
patterns --> hypothetical contexts
relations --> categorical context parsing
metaphoric relations --> cross-domain functions across contexts
specific knowledge --> contextual scope focusing/narrowing

analogies --> applies metaphoric relations to different examples of specific
knowledge for partial transitivity
new knowledge --> modifies existing contexts to incorporate new axioms.
---------- Prioritization and choice in decision systems
(Part of a reasoning engine.)

New action (such as prioritization or actual action)
^---^
Evaluaction ->criteria
^---^
outcome
^---^
choice
^---^
initiative factor(s)
^---^
prioritization
^---^
evaluation-->criteria
^---^
possibilities

Inventing industries with patterns in contexts
    What the world needs more of in order to support the ever rising
population levels, is more industries. An entire industry can be created
simply by developing a new kind of alagorithm, or an algorithm that creates a
niche for people to fill with services or products.
****
An algorithm can be developed by applying an axiom to a new context.
****
This may require forming or describing a new context or kind of context, with
intentions and expectations and attributes or properties in mind, as axoms are
chosen and adapted to make that possible. Theorems can then be derived from
those axioms, that are specific to that context, and when possible, they can
be metaphorically related to theorems in other contexts. This is the basis for
the patterns in contexts model for creating new information. It relates
directly to abdicative reasoning, analogical reasoning, and cross-domain
relations.
    Axioms depend on which dimensions they can exist in and apply to.
For they are the links that connect different dimensions, parts of dimensions,
and sets of dimensions, with the goal of unique lowest-terms representation.
Usually they incorporate at least some implicit knowledge or material
structure in their model.

Property grouping axioms in cross-domain relations.
(See diagram.)
1. All variables have properties.
2. All properties are independent of their variable's context(s).
3. All properties have some combination of qualitative relations, quantitative
relations, existential locations, and existential conditions.
4. Every variable exists within a context and can vary from context to
context.
5. Contexts are composed of networks of patterns, patterns are composed of
networks of variables, and variables are composed of networks of properties.
6. Information can be represented as patterns in contexts, and in that way it
can be represented metaphoricly through analogical reasoning and abdicative

reasoning. Relations of various kinds, location(s), and condition(s) (apon and of) exist at all of the various levels, and those are the data access points.

Today in a Cafe I was talking to my friend -------------- telling him about how I come up with ideas. Besides keeping an ever growing network of questions in the back of my mind, I take a topic or generate a topic by combining keywords, and then think about how that topic is typically represented, then I try to epistemologically dissect that representation and then rebuild the content using different, if not more foundational contextualization of those concepts. Then I go off on a tangent exploring the most interesting parts by associating other concepts, patterns, contexts, and operations to the new representation of the concepts in the original topic.

It is often very valuable to have alternative representations of ideas and concepts and topics because each representation can yield a useful perception. If there is any word sense ambiguity, or use of metaphor, then each alternative representation can yield many perceptions, each of which could uncover previously unseen or unconsidered aspects of the topics, ideas, and concepts. So in the end, exploring and mapping out alternative representations of concepts, ideas, and topics is a way to augment their knowledge base, by generating new perspectives on the information, which can generate entirely new contexts, which can generate entirely new knowledge bases, by treating all information metaphorically. People are currently very good at metaphoric interpretation and analogical reasoning. Computer programs currently are not. It's the next step towards computational methods of abdicative (round-about scenic-route) reasoning.

Anyway, my friend said I should make a program that does what I do, i.e.: a program that recontextualizes information from different perspectives of association, sort of like a choose-your-own-adventure story, but more like a choose-your-own-perspective program. Like a computer program that generates alternative representations of ideas, topics, and concepts. Or even more generally, a computer program that generates alternative representations of patterns (thoughtforms) in a variety of contexts (settings).

Epistemology Systems

Categories, and complete dictionaries as foundations. Quantified objects (and systems) can be juxtaposed into relations that balance alternative representations of objects and systems via a structural or syntactic methodology that acts as a transformation into some of the possible alternative representations of the quantified objects and systems.

Algebras as alternative representations of information. Algebras can rename, or point to representations of information, as well as interconnect and dissect informational objects and systems. All objects and systems are named.

Simulations, recontextualizations, and "polymachines" as alternative models of systems.

Proof is contextual, in other words: proof is dependent on perspective and representation. In much larger contexts than the original context in which something was proven, most "proof" becomes incomplete or uncompatible, and sometimes even false if more foundational epistemological structures are found to have been overlooked. Proof is complete, logically consistent introspection of perceptions of concepts.

Any given proof is only applicable to specific axiom sets. I.E. a proof based on one axiom set may be incomplete or uncompatible or even false in a context composed of a different set of axioms. Therefore concepts must be analogically translated into other contexts and their translations must be formed concurrently with their proof validity in their new context, as a

best-fit categorical search procedure. The proof is a complete, concise
system, so the proof in it's new context can be considered to be a
polymachine, since it is an alternative representation of that system. A
polymachine is a set of cross-domain relations that operate on
analogically-matched patterns from an original context to a new context, and
represents an alternative form of a system in a different context.
    Polymachines are created by inductive, deductive, or (in the case of
analogically translated proofs) abdicative reasoning. Cross-domain
relations
are relations that analogically match the domain of a relation in one context
to the domain of a relation in another context whose range approximates the
same infrastructure and quantitative parameters while leaving the qualitative
parameters categorically open-ended; they are a form of analogical reasoning.
    Input Devices->Internal model buffer->Association and repetition
filter->Analysis/comparison engine->Perceptions on experience->Algebraic
Conceptualization->Character sets and dictionaries, or number systems and
axiom sets -> statements, arguments, inquiries, propositions, implications,
operations, filtrations, combinations, exegesis, dissertation, assignments,
contextualizations, templates, associations, compositions, dissections,
introspections, modifications, adaptations, introductions, translations,
transformations, distortion, refinement, recontextualization, proof,
mapping, search, buffering, sorting, indexing, encoding, decoding,
regulation, pattern formulation, trans-substantiation (joke), frollick.
Copyright 5/23/2005 Justin Coslor
Some definitions for patterns in contexts theory
    Metaphoric objects are informational objects defined by their
relational properties. In relational contexts, sub-contexts of each
property are independent of the application context. Qualitative factors
are computed by mapping and defining a lexicon of their properties.
Qualitative factors are reflective and algebraic usually. Quantitative factors
are computed by counting and performing materialistic operations on them,
and mapping them in that way. Quantitative factors are materialistic and
geometric usually.
Copyright 8/2/2005 to 8/3/2005 Justin Coslor
Cliff Partitions
    Cliff partitions are perceptual references that distinguish deeply layered
patterns from surface patterns, much like a cliff wall bordering the ocean.
In the ocean, every couple of feet down an ocean wall is a new layer, much
like how layers of pixel groups can be laid out on a visual canvas, with some
stacked up several layers high on an edge.
    Cliff partitions are essential markers of where a topology has a steep
slope that may or may not be an overhanging awning above a hidden hollow or
cave. In topology, cliff partitions are useful for analyzing the depth
perception of a view.
    In linguistics, cliff partitions may indicate a sentence that is placed in
the wrong order, or it may indicate a sudden change of topic, or a jump from
one perspective of a context to a deeper or more superficial depth of
perspective of that same context. Cliff partitions in linguistics may also
indicate the boundaries of a given context, where one context ends and another
begins. Cliff partitions are only conceptual perceptual references in
linguistic domains, as writers and speakers linearly paint a nonlinear
picture with their words.
Copyright 5/23/2005 Justin Coslor
Object-oriented processing
    Grids (a.k.a. manifolds), networks, and gridded networks all can house
patterns in contexts of information data sectors as the representation of
knowledge (knowledge is information that contains meaning). Grids, networks,

and gridded networks are materialistic operation spaces for knowledge representation, whereas the notion of "patterns in contexts" are the Platonic operation spaces that form the meaning behind the scenes on the materialistic operation spaces. Identifying the representation of knowledge in an operation space as "patterns in contexts" and specifying the details allows us to work with the information in an object-oriented manner.

Simulated Models and Utility Axioms

If a network or grid is composed of N elements, then it is capable of simulating every possible permutation of those elements by forming internal networks and sub-networks (& grids). Grid networks allow for an infinite number of combinations to be simulated though, but only some simulations are of any use. Maybe there are utility axioms that can be defined to tell us what classes of models contain useful representations. It seems like some factors that might determine whether or not a model is useful would be:

1. Compatibility with existing useful models.
2. Novel representation or novel perspective.
3. Incorporation of new information.
4. Novel capability.
5. Ability to link two or more other models together.
6. Ability to prune other models.

There may be many more factors directly related to evaluating the worthiness of a model. Simulation allows for recontextualization of models and problems and systems.

Operation Spaces continued - Tomographic Data Structures

In the gridded network system, as described previously, a multidimensional array is built between selection of nodes in a network, where elements of this array can be used to build internal networks between the primary node anchors of the array, or between other nodes in other networks --as in cross-domain relations. This process can repeat to an infinite depth, in the order of network node to array anchor to array node to tomographic network to cross-domain relation network to array grid, cyclically. This is a way of creating tomographic data structures of an infinite depth and of infinite permutations, due to the potential for infinite depth, all without adding any extra primary nodes. Every array element and every node represents a relation to or between their anchors or parent nodes.

Operation Spaces: Grids V.S. Networks

Rows and columns and layers are dimensions of a grid, but dimensions can also be parts of an N-dimensional array. Each of the dimensional intersections form a unique partition that relates to or is categorized by it's parent sets' position along their own sequences. So in this way, elemenets on a grid (i.e. in an array) come from multiple parents, wheras elemenets in a network can often come from only one parent (an injective branch). However, in some networks, such as where a planar geometry can exist by the interconnection of more than two nodes, multiple parents can be a grid of subspaces between the nodes on the plane that they make, and in those subspaces multivariable position and quantized quality relations can be said to exist, that are anchored to multiple origin points (each vertex be treated as an origin, and angles between them only serve to define the partitioning of the planar grid). I'll call this kind of transformation of a network "a subspace grid of vertices". Maybe this combination of a grid network can enhance the operation space by making any nodes on a network able to be related to eachother, in grid format, between particular data sections on the subspace grid as well as between other primary nodes.

The other kind of operation space is the Swiss cheese like structure that

surrounds a subspace geometrized grid transformed network. The inner edge of
that space is where one context ends and other contexts may begin to exist.
Copyright 5/14/2005 Justin Coslor
Key axioms and branch axioms in pattern collections.

   Patterns are composed of smaller parts, with the smallest parts being
repetitions of unique elements in which no sub-patterns are apparent; also,
these smallest parts exist and their repetitions make them algebraicly
recognizable due to certain axioms, which act as fundamental truths
(self-evident assumptions) for which no proof is said to be needed.

   This being said, we can say that all patterns that are unique in some
manner must contain at least some unique axioms, and if we look at a
collection of basic patterns and determine what is unique about each one
 and what is in common between them, and then figure out how those
similarities and differences ar ordered on an axiomatic level, we may discover
key axioms and branch axioms which can be represented in a nodal network
graph.

   The value of this is that we can then understand, at the most basic level,
what makes a pattern exist, what makes a pattern recognizable and similar to
other patterns, and what makes a pattern unique.

   We can use that understanding to select axioms suitable to generate a set
of patterns with a measurable degree of flexibility/adaptability, to use
in constructing a system of perception, similar to a painter mixing paints on
an artists pallete, while he mixes concepts in his mind's eye.
Copyright 11/7/2004 Justin Coslor
Hypothetical Relation Highlighting in Undefined Data Sets:

   If categorical names have been assigned to finite elements in a domain,
the rest of the data in the set can be hypothetically considered to be
relations or parts of relations (on those elements and elements not in that
buffered data set). Or they may be elements of categories you don't yet
recognize or know of yet.
9/23/2004 Justin Coslor
Am I reinventing the wheel?

   Today while studying a diagrammatic map on "Can Computers Think?" that
Seth Casana gave me I learned of work that has already been done in Artificial
Intelligence that is very similar to some of the concepts that I came up with
on my own.

   For instance, there has been work done in the area of making computer
software that can understand "analogies". That is very similar to my concept
of "metaphoric operations". Also, in 1989 in seems, Keith Holyoak and
Paul Thagard created ACME, which is a connectionist network that discovers
"cross domain analogical mappings." That soundsd just like my concept of
"cross domain relations for alternative route mathematics", that I have
written about prior to reading anything about it, and I came up with it all on
my own earlier this year. Here are some Analogy Systems:
Copycat - Douglas Hofstadter and Melanie Mitchell 1995.
SME - Brian Falkenhaimer, K. Forbus, and D. Gentner, 1990.
ACME - Keith Holyoak and Paul Thagard, 1989.
8/20/2004 Justin Coslor
Programming

   In the preface to the introductory computer programming book
"The Little Lisper" second edition ISBN 0-574-21955-2 it says: (that in LISP)
"the primary programming activity is the creation of (potentially) recursive
definitions." Now to me, that sounds like the main task (and goal) is to map
out and/or define patterns that are either finite or infinite and to put them
into a relational context that is capable of transforming incoming data
patterns by relating them to stored data patterns, so that the output can be
1. represented, 2. stored, and 3. used/manipulated. I believe this because

nothing is more recursive than a pattern (nothing is less recursive than a pattern as well, except that which is totally random). Patterns always exist within a context or contexts, otherwise they are not recognizable and look like random garbage (see Godel's Theorems). On page vii it also says that "LISP is the medium of choice for people who enjoy free style and flexibility. LISP was initially conceived as a theoretical vehicle for recursion theory and for symbolic algebra." (and likely Lambda Calculus & the EMACS environment for Artificial Intelligence)... LISP syntax looks very similar to my old nonlinear style of thought notation, with its parenthesis within parenthesis (which was good for scaling depth on tangents and concept descriptions).
Copyright 8/4/2005 Justin Coslor
Programming Languages
    "Programming languages are formal languages that have been designed to express computations." - How to Think Like a Computer Scientist - Java Edition
    In other words, programming languages are mappings of balanced processes. The flow of any kind of process can be mapped, if not only approximated by a systematic contextualization of patterns and relations involved in the process. Every system is like a state machine in motion, where the elements and operators are encapsulated by their interconnectivity via contextualization, which is a form of perspective of finite scope.
    Formal languages have fully defined axioms, and are consistent and complete in the mechanics of their methodology. But what is the methodology of mappings of balanced processes in general? The universality concept applies to them: they are consistent and complete because they are balanced about a tight contextualization, where the interconnectivity of the process's elements acts like a fulcrum (when thought of quantitatively), with no element left unconnected. That's why patterns in any context can be transformed through operations into different patterns, so long as there is a method of representing both sets of patterns. The balance comes from having multiple methods of representing each state of the elements in the process. The mapping comes from being able to contextualize the processes, which is only possible if the processes have finite scope, and are completely defined (thus interconnected), and must be systematic (thus logically consistent) in order to be precisely mappable with regularity throughout their states of operation.
Copyright 9/22/2004 Justin Coslor
Patterns In Context Cognition Kernel
[Database]-> [Metabase]-> [Context Rotator]-> [Experiment Application Field]

The following are *a. Subjectively and *b. Objectively
1. Expandable,
2. Adaptable,
3. Translatable, &
4. Summarizable:

Metaphoric Linkers

Pattern Toolkit

Augmentation Socket Parameters
----
*Considerations:

I. Analysis
II. Scope Dimensionality (of input/internal perspective "eyes")
III. Geometry & Quantitative & Qualitative properties of simultaneous

interrupts and their instantaneous functional interrelations and interactions across multivariate sequence states (such as time & symmetry equivalences). **Every set state is but an approximation of the possible combinatorial translations.

Complexity
    Commercial or proprietary software is surjective or injective, but free open-source software is bijective.
    Part of the FRDCSA Tutorial (Free Research Database Cluster Study and Apply) on frdcsa.org says a blurb from an ACM paper about measuring the power of a set of axioms in order to measure the information contained within the set of theorems that can be deduced from those axioms. It says that one can only get out of a axiom sets what one puts in. The paper says something like: "If a set of theorems constitutes t bits of unique information, and the set of axioms that the theorems are based on contains less than t bits of unique information, then it is impossible to deduce those theorems from that set of axioms."
    My friend Andrew J. Dougherty of FRDCSA says that to understand the general necessity of having more software, simply replace "theorems" with "problems", and "axioms" with "programs", and "deduce" with "solve" in the previous statement. Doing that we get: "If a set of problems constitutes t bits of unique information, and a set of programs contains less than t bits of unique information, then it is impossible to solve these problems using just that set of programs. By "problems", I think he means "explicitly defined problems", because an explicitly defined problem is a program that has yet to be executed. Abduction may be necessary to define all of the elements and operators of a problem in the process of turning a problem into a program.
    I say, replace "theorems" with "context", and "axioms" with "patterns", and "solve" with "create". This yields: "If a set of contexts constitutes t bits of unique information, and the set of patterns that the contexts are based on contains less than t bits of unique information, then it is impossible to create those contexts from that set of patterns."
    This is part of my method of knowledge representation for my epistemological representation of artificial intelligence through Patterns in Contexts. Contexts come from patterns that are combined. There can be patterns noticed in the cross-examination of different contexts, but those "patterns" are elements of a greater scope of context than any of the contexts being cross-examined, that is to say, when those cross-context patterns are not noticable when only examining any one of those contexts in relation to itself. This method of knowledge representation may hopefully prove to be useful in the abdicative search for new axioms within and across representable contexts.
A context is represented by its systems of patterns (a.k.a. it's system of axioms).
    New patterns can be discovered by experimenting with data sets: analyzing them in relation to metaphoric operations on other data sets. Metaphoric operations are operations that translate, juggle, predict/locate, and/or transform specified elements across specified contexts.
    New metaphors can be discovered by combining axioms that come from multiple number sets, orderings, and/or algebras. Metaphors are esoteric relations. The application of a metaphoric operation on a data set sometimes results in the discovery of new axioms through the new perspective's set of relations brought about by the application of esoteric relations.
    Metaphoric perception is all about cross-domain relations. This is because

the application of metaphors brings about both:
1. relations between the range of the metaphor and the range of all applicable operations (operations of applications) of the data set, and
2. new cross-domain relations (new domain perspectives) for both the operations of potentially all applications of the data set; and sometimes new cross-domain relations and new ranges for the system and set of relations that algebraically defines the metaphor (when applying the unmatched relations that are not bijective of the operations of applications of the data set) metaphorically (i.e. algebraicly to the metaphor).

Linker patterns

Linker patterns require both an observation buffer (that is at least of equal size to the sum of the contexts to be linked), and linker patterns require an operation buffer that is at least as big as the observation buffer (though far larger is necessary for some observations, even though the amount of data that ends up in the operation buffer may be far less, in some instances, than the amount of data filtered out of the sum of the contexts into the observation buffer).

Data gets filtered out of every applicable context by the linker pattern's "filter specifications", right into the linker pattern's observation buffer. Then the linker pattern's set of metaphoric patterns operates on the observation buffer one at a time or in parallel, but inside the operation buffer.

The linker pattern contains a set of metaphoric patterns whose elements are referenced algebraically to the applicable data elements present in the observation buffer for every possible metaphoric pattern combination present in the linker pattern innately.

Metaphors which are algebraically a complete set of elements to applicable/valid data elements are used in the observation buffer, then inside the operation buffer they perform their calculation (translating, juggling, and/or transforming of the data section by the metaphor) and the linker pattern then places the output in an organized form (so it can be referenced later), and those outputs are placed into a buffer called "the unified context" of the original contexts. This "unified context" includes the linker pattern's filter specifications and metaphor set that was used (i.e. the set that was computable).

Linker patterns can duplicate themselves to divide up the work of applying their metaphoric pattern sets to the observation buffers' data (and they update each other with each successful operation).

Each linker pattern is like a mobile set of operators that copies select groups of contexts and gives birth to unified contexts (which are new contexts). It is each linker pattern's unique set of filter specifications that differentiates one linker pattern from another.

New axioms and theorems that are found elsewhere and within each operation are found and get added to the metaphor set after the valid discovered patterns are provably generalized. They are placed in all of the linker patterns.

Linker patterns can also update each other's set of metaphoric patterns by sharing ones the other doesn't have, and copying new ones from the other.

The observation buffer performs general quantifier type matching.

Patterns In Context Cognition

A context is any specified number set, ordering, or system of numbers that is representative of something (symbolic).

Take the desired outcome (the goal) and break it down into unique aspects. Treat each aspect as an element of a context that contains it, or as an element of several contexts that contain it. each element/aspect may have its own unique context at first. We will be striving to find the pattern or patterns that link all aspects of the goal into one context.

A "linker pattern" can be a linker of the contexts that each of the elements of our goal exist within. Such a pattern links contexts together by assigning a system of translating, juggling, predicting/locating, and/or transforming the specified elements across their specified contexts. This "linker pattern" is metaphoric, and can act as the "unified context" in which we will search for the aspects of our goal, as well as search for alternate routes to each of these aspects (for optimization).

After this experimental search has completed and an optimal cross-domain relation search for shorter routes to each aspect has been completed, we will have generated the optimal route map to our goal.

Cross-domain relations can also be thought of as possible associations, or simply as patterns. They can very explicitly depict ambiguous relationships, such as when they are used with graph theory. Cross-domain relations are a little bit like surjective and bijective networks in logic but where two domains lead to the same range in a number set, even when the domains come from different contexts. They can also be thought of as alternative routes.

Cross-domain relations can be searched for that relate aspects of our goal that are also aspects of goals that have different unified contexts than our goal. It's important to mark the optimal routes out of the cross-domain relations, but keep the other relations (possible routes) for use in future goal structures. By linking multiple goals in this manner, we expand our network of understanding.

Knowledge Mining

Maybe amassing huge intelligent databases that can draw conclusions and make abstractions and predictions towards goals that can recognize & ask for specific data it needs to output one or more units of truth, which could help demystify fields of study and help major breakthroughs occur, if not by simply abstracting and relating so much specific data and general patterns in so many areas; to help bring everything to one's fingertips. A massively parallel search and correlation engine:

The computer has to be able to understand a goal enough to figure out how to better understand that goal, so that it can design it's own searches (determine its own search criteria), and know what a conclusion would look like and would require to be complete enough to make an abstraction.

What is the criteria of a conclusion? Is a conclusion just one particular perspective in every situation? How can the perspective be intelligently shifted and rotated in a search to generate and array of complimentary conclusions? At what point does the difference in goals generate opposing conclusions? (i.e. when do conclusions become apparently contradicting when using the same set of data...) Taking this into account, what difference in goals produces contradictory conclusions (perceptions) when searching (parsing) intersecting sets of data?

Input something like a handbook of chemistry and physics, with a goal of making valid correlations that are not a listed part of that original data set. Start out with general patterns like input types, leading to language semantic patterns, leading to patterns of contextual settings, leading to metaphoric patterns between contexts, *leading to applications of the generalized raw data to the metaphoric patterns, leading to generalized predictions of the outcome of the previous step*, parsing the conclusions listed in the raw data and matching it to the metaphoric mold (the pattern and logic) that led the contained data elements (or equivalents) to that listed conclusion. . .in short: enable the software to understand how the data elements were led to the conclusion listed in the raw data, so that those patterns (metaphoric molds or logic operations) can be understood enough to be

applied to the raw data in different permutations (ways) to uncover
conclusions of previously unconsidered possibilities. Those patterns and
derivation/discovery methods could also be used as a guide for designing
new patterns built from recombining the old patterns with unique data.

And since unique data almost always is unique due to its being composed of
at least some unique patterns; parsing the old (known) patterns from new
(unknown) patterns might make it easier to clarify what exactly the new
pattern is or at least how it operates (or at the very least, its function).
This is knowledge mining. . .One form of artificial intelligence.

Circular Reasoning:

I aught to look up the dictionary definition of a bunch of the key words
in this.. Hey, why not all of the words? A number could correspond to the
number of words the dictionary definition of each word had to reference
(on every level of the tree of lookup words, each branch pausing when it ends
up at it's own word (a loop)) until the parts of the world applicable to the
context of the base word have been described (mapped)), until an upper limit
has been reached on each word. The highest number out of all of the words will
be the number of words in the applicable dictionary to the context of that
paragraph (no repeats). It will be a complete system of circular reasoning.

A complete system of circular reasoning is where every word in a
dictionary is mapped to at least one other word in that dictionary. Some may
be mapped to every word in that dictionary. A complete system of circular
reasoning is one unit. It is aversion/perspective model of a truth. And
different ones can be combined to build complex systems of truth. Like
mitochondria building cells building structures.

Pattern Occurrences

Some patterns are designed or brought about intentionally, and other
patterns are brought about naturally, and others are brought about as an
unintentional consequence of bringing about intentional patterns, such
as in unintentional contexts that are created as a result of layering
patterns, and grouping patterns, and modifying patterns.

Some patterns occur naturally according to certain variable probabilities
specific to their contexts, while others are subject to haphazard creation,
randomness, and free will.

Since all patterns are composed of repetitions, and since the repetitions
are what makes the parts recognizable, and since anything that is recognizable
can be considered a pattern, the reference pieces for the parts of each
pattern can be local, as part of the pattern's context, or the reference
pieces can be remote, as part of other contexts that are accessible to the
perception system. The reference pieces are instances of the repetitions that
make the parts recognizable, and are usually cataloged by order of exposure to
them, as well as by associations.

When new patterns are encountered they are either recognized (thus
categorizable), or they are unrecognizable (thus not categorizable) because
their parts and properties are unknown, or they are partially recognized (thus
potentially categorizable and partly referencable). If the pattern is
new and it is recognized, then its parts are already known but are arranged in
a new configuration and with potentially new properties due to the novel
association of its parts.

So basically, once the perception system is exposed to contexts, the
pattern matching/classification system begins its task of dissecting new
patterns into reference pieces, and classifying recognizable patterns into
association contexts and utility contexts, and assigning priority ratings to
everything so that the perception system can decide what to pay attention to.
Priority ratings get constantly updated, and depend on how much bandwidth and

processing power the perception system and reasoning engine have available.

The reasoning engine does all of the heavy calculations, task and priority assignments, memory management, simulation modeling, and most of the decision making.

ePIC Goal Representation

(ePIC = electronic Patterns In Contexts)

A goal is an abstract construct, and the attainment of a goal is to fill in all of the details of the goal either:

1. in Platonic Reality (information space), or
2. in physical reality (matter configuration space).

If the details have been filled in in Platonic Reality, then the result is a simulation. If the details have been filled in in physical reality, then the result is a working model. A prototype can be a preliminary model or preliminary simulation.

The abstract construct of a goal is the starting point for changing your reality in some way. One need only be able to partially perceive of the abstraction to initiate the existence of the goal, but to fully specify it, a viable plan needs to be formulated. Usually there are unknown variables in every abstract goal, and specifying each variable becomes an iterative process. Often the abstract goal can be stated in the form of a question, and is the result of the questions that arose from some problem. Often times further questioning of the problem impetus is necessary to specify the goal and in doing so, the problem gets solved as the unknowns become decided or calculated.

Many goals are qualitative/categorical subjective/objective priority system calculations, that rely on preference, perspective, universal truths, contextual restrictions, and contextual properties. However, all problems, goals, and solutions can be represented as patterns in contexts, such as undecided patterns in partially determined contexts, that evolve through storing and grouping of categorical, qualitative, and quantitative patterns across different contexts into an experimental buffer/model space towards the sufficiently representative construct or construction of networks of systems of patterns, that satisfy the objectives of the problem and goal, in the context of the final form of the problem and goal.

The Patterns In Contexts concept is an epistemological language, which I strongly believe can be used to represent anything, any concept, and any information of any kind, including first person, second person, third person information in past present or future tense, and it adapts well into any other language.

Cross-Domain Relations in Analogical Relations

A true cross-domain relation would have two domains that each lead to the same range. Analogical relations do something very similar to this, however not quite. In an analogical relation, the relation between the domain and range of one context is mimicked across a somewhat similar domain and range in a different context (only some properties need to be similar for the analogy to be formed, since a barely recognizable similarity needs to exist).

The result is like having generalized an abstraction of the two domains and the relation, and using that abstraction to perform the abstracted relation on the second domain in the other context.

Patterns In Context and Question Asking Systems for Object-Oriented Programming

The patterns in contexts model of knowledge representation and question asking systems based on forming networks of questions and networks of patterns in networks contexts can be used to make a profoundly sophisticated

object-oriented programming system capable of doing analogical reasoning, deductive reasoning, as well as induction and recursions that are simply not representable in other systems. In this system there is a constant acceleration of computational complexity, all of which is progressively designed to simplify the system while augmenting abilities and understanding.
Copyright 5/30/2005 Justin Coslor
    Complexity Progressions
    Every state of a complex pattern can be said to be the result of a progressive augmentation of the previous state or model/version by a new or repeated pattern, or by multiple patterns. That is, unless data loss has occurred due to random deletion or a random addition process.
Copyright 5/31/2005 Justin Coslor
    Pattern Details & Randomness
    Every pattern is the iterative accumulation of modulations and augmentations of sub-patterns, right down to the atomic repetitions that are the first forms that are recognizable from randomness.
    Atomic repetitions may come in a wide variety of non-interoperable modes of partitioning, each of which is subject to a unique perception system that is capable of buffering and filtering its own particular spectrum of atomic repetitions that are partitioned from patterns and randomness that are unrecognizable to that mode.
    Randomness comes in two main forms: there is randomness that is compatible with the partition mode of a given perspective system, thus being countable or measurable via the mathematical comparison of the atomic repetitions of that mode (because it is just a randomization of those atomic repetitions); and the other kind of randomness is composed of randomized patterns that are partitioned in modes other than that which is compatible with the current perspective system.
    It is undecidable whether or not there exists a randomness that cannot be partitioned by any mode of perspective, i.e. a randomness that is not the randomization of some set of patterns or atomic repetitions.
Copyright 9/7/2004 Justin Coslor
    Metaphoric Operations on Patterns Across Contexts
    I want to learn LISP and use it to make an intelligent agent capable of doing metaphoric operations on patterns across contexts.
2/17/2005 Update by Justin Coslor:
    I guess now, most Artificial Intelligence Programming is starting to be done in Java since it is cross-platform and simple to use.
Copyright 9/8/2004 Justin Coslor
    To do this, the sub-agents will need to be able to research raw data configuration sets to look for algebraic repetition that can be considered to be patterns in the sea of cached buffered inputed/observed/recognized elements.
    In order to recognize something, it will have to have a known set of basic recursions (repetitions) to begin with. The prime numbers ar a good source to start out with (since they are the natural balance points in the universe).
    Then it will need to try to describe each data configuration set (data map) whose atomic repetition symmetries can be characterized or parsed. This description will be known as the pattern's type, and patterns with similar types will be grouped into classes.
    To describe a metaphoric operation will require generalizing the differences between each type description in a particular class, and then mapping the observed relations (between each of these types) in the form of a nodal network. That nodal network will be a metaphoric object that summarizes the class.
    Create metaphoric objects for all of the classes in the context (aka

scope) of your total original cached raw data. Then form relations
between different metaphoric objects, and combine and reconfigure
different metaphoric objects, with the original metaphoric objects being
treated as axioms of that particular context. The metaphoric object
relations can be treated as templates for filtering other raw data
contexts in the search for known patterns which contain their own
distinct uniqueness, that will will warrant the generation of new types
in new classes. Every context has its own types in their own classes.
     In other words, every raw data set has its own patterns in their own
contexts. This is how to relate different raw data sets to extract their
relational axioms, and the combination and reconfiguration of different
contexts' axiom sets (metaphoric objects) is what I call metaphoric
operations.
Copyright 8/23/2004 by
Justin Coslor.
Information Theory Quotes
""Metaphor" is a relational model of recursion, where
the circular reasoning (in recursive definitions &
recursive functions) cross-relates the elements of
definitions & functions from multiple (or different)
contexts. That is why cross-domain relations are so
crucial to the metaphoric representation of knowledge
and knowledge systems (logics)."
Copyright 8/26/2004 by Justin Coslor:
"I also believe that information is metaphoric in
nature (has algebraic interconnectivity), and that it
can be represented as a composition of patterns in
contexts, where the contexts themselves can be
patterns, and the atomic elements of each pattern are
composed of symmetry sections (partitions) of data,
where each partition is part of a local or dislocated
repetition (a symmetry, an algebra). And it is only
through the repetition of a data section that part of
a pattern can become recognizable from apparently
random white noise. Randomness and white noise are
probably patterns that are larger than the scope of
our perceptions, so the data appears random. And I say
that metaphors can be represented geometrically
because all of the prime numbers (the balance points
in the universe) are symmetrical when represented
geometrically, and it is likely through primarily
symmetrical sensory and cognitive structures that our
minds can interpret information. And I think of metaphors
not as A = B, but more like the similarity of the
juxtaposition of A's elements in the context of B, and
B's elements in the context of A, in terms of general
systems theory.
I equate truth with workable patterns that become
more and more refined and defined as they get
used. I believe that all truth that we are capable of
perceiving is but a small approximation of the whole
truth. And that the truth/patterns that we are capable
of using is often subject to perception within varying
contexts. But there seem to exist connections between
information none-the-less, through whatever means.
Possibly since (in my opinion) everything came from
oneness)."

Here's another quote from my journal Copyright
11/24/2003 by Justin Coslor:
"Information is a symphony of symbolism and symmetry."
Here's another journal entry Copyright 12/23/2003 by Justin
Coslor:
"Information, by it's very nature, is a division. Yet
it strives to become whole again, and at the very
least, to become balanced."
                           12/25/2004
                    ::Metaphoric Operations::
Metaphors are geometrical, in a sense, that is to say they follow mathematical
geometries. That is to say, metaphors can be thought of in terms of
geometrical patterns and systems. This is because metaphors can be diagrammed,
and diagrams have a relative/nodal/graph-theoretic logic about them, and
through the logic of their patterns and systems they can be recognizable as
having a sort of relational geometry (at least in the unseen
Platonic-reality). Patterns have an algebraic repetition at their foundation,
and the most basic repetitions are symmetries. The most basic symmetries can
be perceived through prime numbers, in that they are the fundamental building
blocks of more complex symmetrical and a-symmetrical structures. A-symmetrical
structures are constructed out of symmetrical structures, just as non-prime
numbers (composite numbers) are constructed out of prime numbers and
relations/functions. Metaphoric operations are relational templates that are
axiomatic, adaptable, reconfigurable, and versatile. This is because they are
collections of relations whose options have been generalized to optimize those
qualities for relating similar, and different qualitative domains across
contexts. Each context's qualities' relations are unique to that context's set
of axioms. One might say that domains are qualitative, while the domain's
ranges can be qualitative OR quantitative. Metaphoric operations relate
different consistent, recursively complete, contexts by copying or moving
elements from each context into the separate but more versatile context of the
metaphoric template. Once the elements have leave their original context,
their original context's axiom set(s) may be altered, as well as some of the
context itself (and sub-contexts, if any are relevant). Metaphoric contexts
may only need to copy some of the axioms of their element's original contexts,
because they have axioms of their own that help to allow for the relation of
the axioms that are buffered in from multiple other contexts. The metaphoric
template's original axioms also help to relate the qualitative elements which
are the current primary focuses, that were constructed out of relevant axioms
from the external contexts. New knowledge is created when the qualitative
elements' axioms sets are adapted to form new qualitative elements and
relations out of the augmentation of the metaphoric template's context's axiom
sets, by the elements' external axiom sets. With metaphors, anything that
isn't explicitly cross-domain related is ignored. Qualities are itemized as
they are noticed or as they are deemed relevant. Personally, I feel like the
diagram of metaphoric operations is a lot prettier than the description...
Copyright 12/25/2004 by Justin M. Coslor
Copyright 1/9/2005 Justin Coslor
Visual Dictionaries and Axiomatic Abdicative Simulations
    Maybe as part of building the logical framework for a systematic visual
dictionary, we could try representing each image both as a set of angular or
situational perspectives; but also I think it's important to try to axiomatize
the image properties into contexts, and by doing so we can do abdicative
creative constructions (and abstractions of those to some approximate goals),
such as by perceiving each image as a series of nodes (graph theory vertices)
and connections that are all linked together both contextually in the physical
space, and conceptually in the historical-timeline/platonic interaction space.

By doing this, the heuristic (guess-work) training can be semi-automized and the intelligence data on the scenario objects can have a far deeper meaning and farther reaching applications. Deepening the understanding of content and its abdicative recombinations and metaphoric transcombinations, both increases the potential for creating new applications and tools, and increases the versatility and effectiveness of existing tools and applications. Deepening understanding of content creates new contexts and reconceptualizes stuff by augmenting axiom sets that the contexts are based on.

Axiomatic Visual-Layer Interpretation

Forming stronger linkages between axiom sets deepens the meaning of content of all structures that are based on those axioms. It can also complicate things by cluttering the contexts that those structures act within if the linkages are formed sub-optimally. Such is the case of an image with ambiguous layering. This has applications to steganography, computer vision, and virtual-reality educational environments, etc.

Patterns In Contexts: 3D Engine

I think Java3D, combined with some inexpensive virtual reality equipment, will be the ideal environment for exploring Patterns In Contexts theory visually. Critical to that is a software that is able to parse video data into 2D objects and build 3D geometric reconstructions of those objects along with the parameters of their observable range of motion, and do heuristic guessing at the backsides of the objects that are hidden from view or just make the 2D objects into 3D avatars that always face you regardless of which side of theme you are on. That way, video data can be geometerized and represented as Patterns In Contexts, and 3D worlds can much more easily be created by mixing together objects and behaviors from an enormous archive of experience (from video sources) that is all parsed and sorted categorically by a visual dictionary that maps adjectives and nouns and verbs to pattern properties such as qualitative geometric relations, axiomatically defined variables and operations, and contextually associated references of objects and their pattern groupings. Each entry of the visual dictionary will contain an up-to-date list of all objects in the pattern archive that contain the geometric or otherwise visual property defined by that visual dictionary entry. Scale, color, orientation, state, position, and quantitative data in many cases can be ignored by the visual dictionary, unless the entry is directly intended to describe one or more of those properties.

Graphical Representation and Visual Heuristics

Make a website loaded with graphs, diagrams, flowcharts, and simplified geometric reconstructions of stuff, events, places, flows, tools, intellectual understanding, interpretations and translations, programs, systems, etc. Call it "mapworld" or "graphworld." Make webcrawling intelligent agents that generate extensive thorough, and systematic visual dictionaries online.

Similarly, there should be a webpage utility where you can enter the URL (Uniform Resource Locator = website address) to some text or copy/paste in some text directly and it could try to abstract visual perceptions of the text content's meaning and represent it in the form of a diagram or graph, etc. It could also try researching images on the internet that are related to the text. I realize that the second part might be difficult, since there aren't very many visual dictionaries in existance yet, and computer vision and machine learning technologies may not be that advanced yet (but maybe they are...?). Heuristics (guess-work on visual data and in language processing is just a matter of logical deduction, manual training of Bayesian statistical and Connectionist techniques, and

metaphoric/analogical/cross-domain-relational mappings across contexts,
to bridge systems not yet adapted to each other.

Creativity & Understanding

Language is permutations of semantics, governed by syntax and context,
with meaningful intention.
So....
What is the language of creativity?
What are its semantics?
What is its syntax?
What is its context?

The language of creativity always contains either:
1. new semantics or new permutations of semantics, and/or
2. new syntax, and/or
3. new context.
*Creativity does not always convey meaningful intention.

The semantics of creativity are new patterns and/or old patterns thought
of in new ways (recontextualized patterns). The syntax of creativity is
either internally defined by the language of the format (if the format is
known), or else (if the format is new) it is externally defined by the
naturally occurring partitions and connections of the organic objects and
systems of developments of the natural universe, or by the connections and
partitions present in the diagonalizations of synthesized patterns juxtaposed
through a relational operator or operation, and/or the diagonalization of the
juxtaposition of synthesized patterns and natural patterns juxtaposed through
a relational operator or operation, and/or the diagonalization of the
juxtaposition of natural patterns juxtaposed through a relational operator or
operation.

The context of creativity is always at least partially new. Creative
expressions composed entirely of entirely new patterns (not just modified
ones) in entirely new contexts with external syntax that has never before been
known of and that is unrelatable to known syntax will always appear random and
entirely undecipherable unless the person or interpretation program is capable
of analogical abdicative reasoning. However there will be no conclusive
proof
that the analogies drawn will be correct. The analogies may be qualitatively
correct in the metaphoric sense, but they will never be proven quantitatively
correct to the knowledge of the analyst. There has to be some decoding method,
key, or common ground known to the analyst in order to decipher such a
creative expression.

Concepts
Layers of states and states of layers (As in "finite element state
machines" and similar systems):
^^^^^^^^^^^^^^^^^^^^^^
Art
Video
Writing
Talking
Scent
Taste
Touch

Mathematics -> connections and differences in maps of possibilities
Philosophy -> depth of possibility maps models of truth progressing
Science and Technology -> exploration of possibilities through careful
experimentation and adaptation to discoveries

Can you think of more? It is definitely possible.
Look for stuff like those descriptions. Juxtapose operators and
abdicatively
reason into applications.
Measurement Systems
    In measurement, two or more quantities or qualities are compared to one
another, such as a unit of measure applied to a starting point and ending
point of another object. When a unit of measure is undefined, you look for the
minimum unit(s) of commonality between the objects and mark the overlap points
and the center-points between the starting and ending points, and the center
points between those points, etc. If any number systems or other patterns are
used as division or counting units (such as prime numbers), as well as
center-point binary tree parsing, we realize that "all measurement is really
comparison by parsing or partitioning". The units of the partitioning or
parsing can be native common denominators of the observer's perception system
and the object.
    The intersection of the juxtaposition of multiple objects is another
native unit of parsing, which itself can be parsed into smaller units via a
number system or other pattern. Common ground or compatibility is necessary
for comparison, and since measurement is a form of comparison, measurement is
an act of perception adaptation via parsing or partitioning. It's the act of
trying to perceive of an object via the perception system of something
else, and often times perception systems miss a lot because there are often
lots of valid ways for a particular observer to perceive of things, and it's
an undecidable problem about whether a perception system is not recognizing
other undefined potential aspects of the object, let alone know what it is not
perceiving through its axioms and atomic units of partitioning, and methods of
parsing and grouping, and methods of determining anchor points,
interpretation, starting and ending points, edge detection, pattern layering,
and buffer sizes and contextualization, etc.
    Active measuring is when ea system's partitioning structure and
methodology/reasoning system is constantly updated as something is being
measured. An example of active measuring is a system capable of learning, such
as an adaptive or evolutionary perception system, such as an artificially
intelligent reasoning system or human being. A perception system that is
merely adaptive but not evolutionary is autonomous or semi-autonomous, but not
intelligent, since it only knows the context that it currently exists in. By
storing perception systems adapted to multiple contexts, a system can then
often map out the commonalty and differences between each context and form a
general common-sense perception system which can be analyzed inductively,
deductively, and abdicatively by its reasoning engine.
    Analysis via comparison of the domains and ranges of functions that exist
in different contexts is an abdicative reasoning process since it is a
form of
analogical reasoning. Once again common ground must be mapped between the
functions being compared or else an external perception system will have
to artificially map its units onto both functions so that compatible parsing
and partitioning can proceed in a measurable, if not blind (thus artificially
simulated) representation.
    Passive measuring is when the measurement and perception system's
reasoning engine is not updated by internal induction, deduction, or abduction
during measurement, nor after measurement. Passive measurement is merely
mechanical and not adaptive or evolutionary.
    Re-contextualized Patterns

It's interesting how patterns and their implications change as their raw data is re-contextualized and/or perceived from different perspective systems and contexts. The parameters of each context shapes the possibilities of its patterns' applications, implications, and recognized states of existence.

Often times the possibilities of contexts overlap, and are subjective in the sense that there may exist several possible ways to perceive of and interpret a context, where each way may have equal or varying levels of probable truth in its systems, depending on the perspective system and intentions/expectations of the observer and/or the controller.

Observing patterns and differences

Combining my poem about "Sight" with my poem about "Reasoning Engines", leaves me thinking about the line "from color comes shape" and the line about "thinking as storing and grouping knowledge", and how it takes a pattern to perceive of a pattern, such as one colored shape outlining or juxtaposing against another colored shape, and how each of these shapes (and color information) gets stored as a piece of knowledge (a pattern), and how both are grouped together by their situational context. The differences between them are patterns not origininally apparent in either piece of knowledge prior to their comparison, unless those patterns are stored in the perceiver's virtual knowledge base from prior experience or innate programming.

So you can try grouping every atomic pattern with every other atomic pattern (time allowing), and as long as you're working with more than a one-dimensional medium, the differences between each atomic pattern being compared one-to-one will constitute a unique atomic pattern. This sort of comparison is one way of coming up with new knowledge in mediums that exist in two-dimensional (or greater) qualitative and/or quantitative and/or conditional mediums, and mediums that combine different types of properties.

* Comparing unequivalent objects always creates partitions in either one or both of the objects. The remainder partitions are sometimes entirely knew but virtual objects. *

"Sight"
From color comes shape,
and from shape comes size,
we triangulate images
that come into our eyes.

"Reasoning Engines"
1. Knowledge as patterns in contexts.
2. Thinking as storing and grouping knowledge.

----

* Language contextualizes perceptions. The language used in each perception identifies and indicates patterns that have been parsed through comparison. *

Pattern Matching

Previously I've written about how if you divide a circle into a bunch of equiangled sectors and if there is a prime number of sectors then no symmetrical alternating coloring patterns exist, but if there is a non-prime number of these equiangled sectors, then you can color in alternating sectors or groups of sectors to form symmetrical patterns that correspond to each of the composite number pieces.

To apply this to pattern matching, simply cut the circle so that its sectors lie in a straight line and then look at the coloring patterns to match pieces of that linear pattern to strings of numbers, where each color might be a particular number, or just do it in binary. In this manner you can make numerical landmarks in raw data streams to look for patterns within potentially random data.

When only a piece of one of these composite number symmetry patterns shows up in a linear data stream, that may indicate that other layers of patterns may be overlapping it. The thing that makes these patterns recognizable from randomness is the juxtaposition of their unique alternating prime partition patterns. An individual prime partition pattern piece that has been linearized is indistinguishable from any other linear prime partition pattern piece unless you know for sure that you're seeing the whole thing. But when you juxtapose two or more of these patterns together in the form of a composite symmetry pattern even a fragment of that pattern can dramatically narrow down the possibilities of its origin. Copyright 6/20/2005 Justin Coslor Remote-Controlled Contexts Via Preprocessor Switchboards (See Diagrams)

Instead of having injective, surjective, and bijective, maybe there could be a preprocessor module that is bijective that goes in front of all surjective and injective relations. For a surjective relation: P1 = surjective ARP1 = bijective ARB = surjective = ACP1B For an injective relation: ARP2 = bijective P2RB = injective ARB = injective = ACP2RB A and B are domains P1 and P2 are preprocessors R is a relation, C is a cross-domain relation.

In effect, the preprocessor becomes a duplicate of the domain element in A, but independent of the context of A. So since the preprocessing is done outside of A, you can have single-line inputs from A, and you can take several domain elements out of their contexts and perform their relations via remote control.

In the second diagram, the cross-domain relation BCP2 is turned off, so context D doesn't contain its relation (P2RD) unit P2 gets turned back on. In that diagram, D is a remote-controlled context via the preprocessor operations switchboard S.

A, B, and C are each in their own contexts and they combine in context D. The preprocessor modules allow for simple remote control like an operations switchboard. Copyright 6/12/2005 Justin Coslor Definitions

Defining something by cataloging it's properties and relations is blind unless you specify the particular context of the thing, and the sub-contexts of the properties and relations it is composed of. Context is both an exoskelletal structure as well as an endoskelletal structure. Context is is defined by both the external limits as well as the internal limits. Copyright 6/5/2005 Justin Coslor Geometric Abstractions When doing abstraction on geometries and photos of patterns (symmetry formations, repetitions of patterns, and that which is recognizable from randomness), maybe all that is needed is a map of intersection points for each level of connectivity: i.e. a map of all points where two lines intersect, a map of all points where three lines intersect, etc. The union of all of those maps should form a sufficient geometric abstraction to recreate a recognizable approximation of the original model of photo patterns. Copyright 6/4/2005 Justin Coslor Index of Topics *(Remember to finish adding topics to this index, as it is only a partial list of ePIC-related topics I've written about so far.) choice creativity patterns contexts variables properties relations: quantitative, qualitative, cross-domain, analogical abstraction models simulations axioms: key, branch knowledge: implicit, explicit, representation intuitions complexity progressions pattern details randomness analogical recursions question asking systems question expectation templates object-oriented processing operation spaces: grids v.s. networks analogy metaphor examples Copyright 6/4/2005 Justin Coslor Abstraction

Abstract relations are relations described by descriptions that are

the simplified form of lexicons, where the details have been stripped
and only the categorical data remains, along with some quantitative data
(possibly. . .I'm not sure yet....), such as the dimensions and data
types. Relations are fairly easy to abstract because you can just build
an itemized list of the operators and verbs used on or in the general
context of the domains that use them. Copyright 6/3/2005 Justin Coslor
(See example diagrams) If a domain A is cross-domain related to a domain
B analogically, that relation can be injective, or subjective; or if it
is bijective, even if it's bijective to another element in the domain
than the starting point, then we can say that the relation is recursive.
This is an example of analogical recursions, because since all bijective
relations are recursive, and analogical reasoning deals primarily with
cross-domain relations, then all cross-domain relations that are
bijective are analogical recursions. Another form of cross-domain
analogical recursions comes from alternating back and forth through a
set of relations between two or more domains, where the active element
in the active domain is determined by some function on the ordering of
the elements in that domain (a sequence function on the cardinality).
Injective analogical recursions can also exist in a back and forth
system that ultimately loops between the various domains of two or more
contexts. Copyright 5/25/2005 Justin Coslor Implicit V.S. Explicit
Knowledge

   In knowledge bases, facts and data are stored in patterns and
contexts explicitly, but that same information may also belong to other
contexts, and can be arranged into different patterns and may have
unidentified relations to patterns in that data set and/or to patterns
not in that data set.
   Often times there are multiple hierarchical levels and recursions of
patterns in contexts and sub-contexts in patterns, and bridging across
these levels are more of the same in many cases. Data that is implied
can be treated as though it is hidden, though its role may be very
important in the context of the data that depends on it. In the
perception of questions, lots of implicit patterns and contexts are
necessary to generate and adapt simulated models of the knowledge that
is involved with the possible ways to represent the meaning of the
question, as well as for generating models of the expectation parameters
of the context templates involved with goal search, answer retrieval,
and answer formulation (for discovering or constructing suitable content
of the right level of detail). This is because every question is the
intersection of multiple contexts, or rather every question is an
attempt at adapting multiple contexts into compatibility, and thus
unknowns must be declared. Copyright 5/16/2005 Justin Coslor Analogy,
Metaphor, and Examples Now due to my lack of a dictionary on hand I'll
create some of my own definitions (the names can be changed later). An
analogy is like half of a metaphor. An analogy gives an elaborated
example of a relation, whereas a metaphor gives an example of a relation
across multiple contexts (a cross-domain relation). An example of an
analogy is like saying: An apple is like an onion. Both rot, and are
edible. An example of a metaphor is: Apple is to onion as postman is to
salesman. An analogy is essentially a simile plus a moral or
explanation/elaboration. A metaphor may describe the same relation(s) as
an analogy in that it juxtaposes two or more pieces of information. This
is similar to generating a unique diagonal length from a box generated
by using one sequence or variable quantification as the x axis and
another sequence or variable quantification as the y axis to produce a
unique qualitative variable or sequence... Add more dimensions to the
diagonalization to combine more variables or sequences or functions...

Then just rotate the diagonal axis until it is horizontal. But metaphor goes a step farther and presents another example of that relation, but in a different context. *Examples are contextualizations of patterns. A relation between qualitative variables is thus a diagonalization of their quantitative mappings. In this way, qualitative mappings can be represented geometrically. Patterns are composed of variables and relations between variables. **Variables are usually qualitative property sets that have been quantitatively mapped into juxtaposition with their enumerated algebraic repetitions. Juxtaposition via diagonalization is a form of an operator. ***Operators are forms of juxtaposition of variables and patterns. Addition sequentially juxtaposes variables and patterns on a grid. Subtraction is the opposite of addition, as it removes variables and patterns from a grid. Multiplication sequentially adds to columns of categories, one category at a time. Division de-references and parses columns of categorical values, and is the opposite of multiplication. Addition, subtraction, multiplication, division, 2D geometry, trigonometry, algebra, calculus, etc, ... all are operations that can be performed on a grid. Change the operation space (i.e. change the context), and the axioms that these operations are based on may no longer apply; but some may, and those are the axioms we want to collect for a wide range of adaptability, and can be used in forming general systems theory grids and networks.

As far as I know about operation spaces, there are grids and there are networks. Each can be within each, they can come in many different forms, and translations are possible between them, but the translation between a grid and a network always relies on a core set of axioms that are in common between the two data structures. Copyright 5/4/2005 Justin Coslor (Based on a theory I had around the year 2000) Sight -------- From color comes shape, and from shape comes size, we triangulate images that come into our eyes. ------------------------- Fall 2001 to 4/25/2003 Justin Coslor My fundamental theorem of Computer Vision: I believe that from color comes shape and from shape comes size; comparatively/relatively/contexually. I'll have to read about the cognition of vision to fill in the details and check out software and plasticware/firmware/hardware models of visual perception. Learn known mathematical techniques. Copyright 5/6/2005 Justin Coslor Rules Are Behavioral Expectations Here are some types of rules: Laws, priorities, environmental limitations (physics), trends, norms, common sense, personal limitations, societal beliefs, personal beliefs, lazy tendencies & optimizations, conditions, terms of use or license agreement, policy, ethics, morals, probability judgments, priority judgments, game theoretic strategy, preemptive negotiation, real-time negotiation, post hoc proc negotiation, design considerations, navigational control, pattern guidelines, pattern maps, mathematical modeling and calculation, combination possibilities, case-by-case possibilities; forum dimensionality, axioms, theorems, and restrictions; units and parsing and sorting methods and requirements; activation, deactivation, and flow control theory, network access methods, network exchange methods, network dynamics. Here are some qualifiers for those kinds of rules: Global, situational, regional, local, continuous, temporal, static, dynamic, linear, parallel, hierarchical, symmetric, independent, context specific, general, intentional, unintentional, conscious/unconscious, automatic, manual, modal, type, categorical. Find an ontology that lists concepts related to a given concept, in a hyper-linked format. Similar to encyclopedia references (see Wikipedia.org) or book topical references in the public library's card catalog. Copyright 1/7/2005 Justin Coslor Categories: Part 1 Even if

categories get proven to be inaccurate (*Are accuracy proofs based on
any subjective information?), then useful information about the
compatibility of the data elements can be discovered as parameters get
refined. Ultimately, it is the compatibility of the elements, both in
and between data sets, that makes the fundamental definitions of the
categories. Copyright 11/7/2004 Justin Coslor Hypothetical Relation
Highlighting in Undefined Data Sets: If categorical names have been
assigned to finite elements in a domain, the rest of the data in the set
can be hypothetically considered to be relations or parts of relations
(on those elements and elements not in that buffered data set). Or they
may be elements of categories you don't yet recognize or know of yet.
Guessing about Neural Architectures... This is a journal entry,
Copyright 9/12/2004 by Justin Coslor.

I could be totally wrong about this, but it is currently presumed,
by me at least, that neural architectures tune to, receive, translate,
and transmit various wavelengths of patterned energy configurations. The
tuning functions may be in one unit, the receivers/input devices may be
in another unit; the translation/manipulation apparatus may be in
another unit; the translation/manipulation apparatus may operate in a
unit of its own, and the transmission/re- communication apparatus may be
in a unit of its own as well.

There is likely data loss in the imperfections and limitations of
the tuning apparatus, the receiving apparatus, and the re-transmission
apparatus successively; however, the translation/manipulation apparatus
may apply experience-based heuristics to fill in the holes and sharpen
or simplify the distortions and puzzles in the data field. Each cluster
of nodes, as well as the relation nodes themselves sometimes perform
negotiations for syntactic and semantic consistency. Such negotiations
are likely interfaces composed of multi-purpose reconfigurable general
cellular nodes. Meaning might be derived from information streams by
creating translations and equivalence representations in other classes
and other contexts, and by defining and rating utility functions and
organizing them in such a way that their priority can easily be
determined relevant to the general function of the class of relations
they belong to in generalized/easily-specialized contexts. The neat
thing about information, rather than cause and effect, is that it can be
re-conceptualized and re-contextualized and re-framed/re-patterned.
10/22/2004 Justin Coslor (after reading pg. 11 %ÛÍModern Algebra%Û? by
Gilbert and Vanstone) Some methods of Proof: - Assumptions (context) -
Examples of problems or experience - Critical questions of interest -
Representative language choice -Translation/Mapping -> same or different
context? - Inventory of context axioms - Define critical question's
search scope - Assume all questions are somewhat answerable - Convert
other knowledge into current representation and abstract relationships
without regard to hierarchical depth - Group compatible relationships -
Mark partial compatibilities as overlapping sub-contexts - Hypothesize
mappings that assume each relationship to be the answer to a series of
questions - Look for hypothesized questions similar to questions of
interest - If found, remap original examples in terms of those similar
mappings of hypothesized questions - Define inconsistencies and address
them - Represent conclusion - Explore relations of conclusion to other
contexts - Blah blah blah, I should study more. 8/12/2004 Justin Coslor
Axiom Notes (Here are some note I took at the public library today.)
Structuring XML Documents / David Megginson CLP MAIN SCI&TECH QA76.76H94
M44 1998 The National Strategy To Secure Cyberspace February 2003
http://www.gpoaccess.gov - Perhaps people and machines should be trying
to prove the limits of proof. - There are many shapes of non-Euclidean

geometric reality. - Perhaps quanta of energy is a form of matter that exists on non-Euclidean spiral and tubular planes? Maybe quanta breaks off from matter and electrons that exist on non-Euclidean spherical planes during orbit changes and altitude changes? I read part of the end of the book Thinking about [TLC] LOGO: A graphic look at computing with ideas. pg. 206&207 ISBN 0-03-064116-0 Each set of axioms is based on a unique working model of the universe. (Regardless of the completeness of the model.) In many cases, there is some overlap between different sets of axioms, because many contexts have some properties and/or patterns that are in common. Metaphoric operations describe the relations between the properties and/or patterns that are in common between unique contexts. More than that, each set of axioms attempts to define a working model of the universe, and that no model of the universe is complete (hence it is a model) other than the universe itself; and from within the universe, a model of the universe can only be approximated, and to a varying degree of accuracy and/or applicability at that. 8/20/2004 Justin Coslor Update: So essentially, a set of axioms is only as good as the model they attempt to describe. Copyright 6/8/2004 Justin Coslor Contexts

A context is a relation that defines a group of patterns. A pattern that is not related to any other patterns is isolated, and can for the most part be considered "invisible" to other contexts. A context can also be considered to be a pattern, and can sometimes also be considered as subject to this "isolation" concept. Patterns that exist within networks of contexts are the most easily located, since cross-domain relation-based experimental search and discovery methods need not be applied to locate or define them, as is necessary in many cases to find isolated patterns (i.e. island knowledge). Networks can consist of relations (surjective, injective, and bijective) and cross-domain relations (which are potentially multi-node route reverse-surjective relations). Data turns into knowledge as the patterns and contexts and networks of contexts are mapped out. Copyright 6/5/2004 Justin Coslor Perception

Every multi-state organization or cognitive organism exists on a higher plane than it is capable of perceiving, because nothing can monitor every aspect of itself (unless every cell is symmetrically identical) since the monitoring devices (sensors, etc), even when recursive, cannot monitor every aspect of themselves. This is because in order to perceive of something we must classify it in terms of something else we have perceived, and since we were born in motion, our consciousnesses pass forward from state to state, processing information (perceiving of things in terms of the physical universe) until parts, or the entirety of our bodies have fully ceased to move (i.e. until the breakdown of the subparts).

As Godel's theorem implies: "no set can map its powerset". After some developed mental subparts have broken down, the structures of the consciousness that they were physically translating may continue to operate outside of the rest of the brain's physical time-frame. The latency of the various cognitive architectures in the brain may have a great deal to do with the relativistic self-observations of multi-sensory experiences. Since after all, some parts of the mind/body connection and mind/brain connection operate at near the speed of light (as electrons flow between the parts of each cell). Copyright 8/10/2005 Justin Coslor Perception -- continued from 6/5/2004.... On 6/5/2004 I wrote that "The latency of the various cognitive architectures in the brain may have a great deal to do with the relativistic self-observations of multi-sensory experiences." In other words, people

think at different rates and depths from time to time, and that can
create recall and encoding obstacles in grouping and interfacing
memories between different cognitive states. However, those kinds of
qualitative and quantitative differences between the contents of
memorized perceptions can create bridges into depthier re-perceptions
for recognition into fine- tuned contexts. 5/17/2003 Justin Coslor A.I.
Notes Today I did a http://Google.com search on OpenCYC
     Thought Treasure V.S. OpenCyc came up. I guess both are major
knowledge base ontology management systems, i.e. Reasoning Engines.
     Thought Treasure seems to have more stuff for Natural Language
Processing than OpenCyc, but it is only free for noncommercial use. The
Cyc technology though is the world's largest and most complete general
knowledge base and commonsense reasoning engine. The CIA uses it, and
did about 500 man-years worth of data-entry into to. OpenCyc is a much
smaller subset of Cyc, and is open-source.
     Cycorp runs opencyc.org, and also makes ResearchCyc for R&D in
academia and industry. Dependencies: none Languages: CycL, SubL, Java
(other API's on the way) Platforms: Linux (Win32 coming soon) Sites:
http://opencyc.org foundry.ai-depot.com/Project/OpenCyc /Amygdala /Fear
/GAUL /Joone /LogicMoo /OpenAI /SigmaPi /Simbrain 10/20/2004 Justin
Coslor Mission Statement
     Free open-source software is quite possibly the best hope, in
conjunction with the freely accessible Internet, to give the common
citizens a fighting chance at building foundations for their decendents
in the midst of the mechanized empires of greed that thwart and encroach
on their liberties and livelihoods in their attempts to squeeze and
control the creative potential of supposedly free individuals who might
otherwise be nurtured to blossom as citizens of a humbly selfless and
harmonious planet Earth, that we all know can happen.

                                Book II:
                          Networks of Questions

========================
Everything I know about questions.
========================
By Justin Coslor
justincoslor@gmail.com
     (These ideas are all copyright by Justin Coslor on their respective
dates. I very much want to share these ideas, but I want to work in
collaboration on related projects, so I withhold all intellectual
property rights to this material. The work in this document is just a
small selection of my ideas. Please do not steal my work via Tempest
equipment or by any other means. If you are interested (due to tempest
surveillance since I haven't shown anyone this,) and wish to
collaborate, feel free to contact me at the above email address, and I
will keep your technological secrets as long as you don't exploit me.
Also, I'm egalitarian and I don't build weapons. Let's get that strait.
Realize, I'm living on food stamps and measley disability stipend that
barely pays the rent.) 2/28/98 Standard Inferences About actions: who
what happened why when where how. Most everything else just uses one or
a couple of these inferences. 10/6/2003 Query As far as questions are
concerned... It seems like there are yes/no questions, option questions,
spectrum questions, ind-depth (and short) descriptive questions,
computational questions, essay questions, etc. Some are subjective (of
opinion), some are neutral, some are definitive, some are explanatory,
some are geometrical/visual, some are mathematical, some are of finite

domain, some are impossible, some are biased, some are traps, some are falsely/inaccurately stated, some are open-ended, some are meaningless/pointless, some are direct, some are indirect, some are of infinite domain (a snapshot), some are time/space sensitive, some are quantitative, some are qualitative, some are recursive. 8/1/2004 Questions (a re-write) Questions can be used to define agendas; or indicate knowledge; gaps; or inquire about attributes, associations, and relations; or speculate; or to demonstrate something or make a statement; or be used for introspection or inspection; or to infer, deduce, or search for the elements of a pattern or context or its system(s) or relations; or to map assumptions (an assumption being the context that defines a set of beliefs); or to analyze and re-analyze data and information. 3/15/2005 Networks of Questions

In considering ideas and information that is new to me, I ask networks of questions. The questions can be framed as dependency charts. Now what is a good way to understand dependency charts? List out the major nodes (most well-connected nodes) as open-ended definitions, and form lexicons out of the interconnected definitions. Next map out the rest of the nodes axiomatically using those definition structures. Turn this into a software for common sense perception. Maybe make a web crawler cognition engine that can learn the meaning behind things so that it can solve problems by figuring out new ways of thinking about things (adapting the context of question/perception networks). 3/15/2005 Experimentation Sometimes experimentation is necessary to solve problems and answer questions, because some nodes of information or questions or contextual perception networks are otherwise unreachable, and often entirely unknown to exist. 4/15/2005 Question Networks, continued... Abdicative reasoning: When does a function discover or prove an axiom? What metric makes analogy recognizable? Do recursive lexicons have the potential for infinite macro-scale growth? Do they have the potential for infinite micro-scale growth? Or will they all be governed primarily by the initial categories? Form networks of questions to gain valuable perspectives on topical and problem data. Model question engines in a careful evolutionary goal manner with substainability and capability and necessity as the primary objectives. Map the spectrum of inquiry. Expectations->Intentions->Experimentation (scientific combinations)->Dependency Chart Gaps and Representation Gaps->Formulation of questions incorporating "known" data. 5/4/2005 Answers We're surrounded by answers, but they're all meaningless and often impossible to even detect without knowing at least some of the questions that they are derived from. Without this question/answer connection, there is no consciousness, awareness would not exist. Copyright 5/10/2005 Justin Coslor Re-defining basic question thought-forms: Why? = Is there a reason for how this came to be, and what is it? What? = The existence of this shall be called by a name that needs to be defined, and we are inquiring about that. When? = This occurred or shall occur at what time and day? How? = By what process does this function? Notice that I had to use "what" in every one of these (except I tried not to use "what" in it's own definition, which was difficult). Therefore "what" is the most important thought form to focus on. "What" is the algebraic domain of the relation "that", or "this", or "these", or "those"; and the range is unknown, and is entirely unbounded. "That", is a pointer to a specific instance of something in existence (whether it be in physical or Platonic reality). The difference between Platonic objects and physical objects is that Platonic objects are just pointers to other pointers, whereas physical objects are pointers that point to themselves in a loop. Physical

objects can bound and/or link (like a chain) other physical objects
because if we geometrize the representation of the pointers we have
physics, since the pointers loop. We exist partially in physical
reality, and partially in Platonic reality since we can make conversions
between the two. It's like the difference between particles and waves.
Copyright 6/17/2005 Justin Coslor Question Networks: Option questions
v.s. spectrum questions

A lot of ambiguity is in every question. For instance, if you asked
a question today you'd get one answer most likely, but if you asked that
same question 10,000 years from now you'd probably get a much different
answer. The scope of a question can be narrow or it cana be wide. With a
narrow scope, a question might be a basic question that can be modified
by many options, or it can be a bunch of cases, as in specific
questions. Those are option questions. They lay out perspective question
options.

When the scope is very general or comprehensive of a lot of
possibilities, then it is a spectrum question because it is intended to
explore a range of possibilities that are within the same domain. Option
questions seek to explore multiple questions that are not necessarily of
the same domain. Copyright 5/25/2005 Justin Coslor Question expectation
templates and question context intersections

Questions contain an expectation template of the kind or class of
answers that thet inquisitor is looking for. Often times though, the
answers that are found or generated, or the answers that are of the most
use, do not match the question's expectation template. Often times,
answers that ar suitable cannot be derived or located until the question
is elaborated, generalized, or otherwise modeled using different
representation, such as analogical equivalencies of its objects,
objectives, contexts, and relations.

Every question is the intersection of several contexts, where behind
the scenes, each context has its own unique expectation template; such
as: - 1. The type of question: who, what, where, when, why, how, and its
structure and methods. - 2. The semantic purpose of the question
indicated by the question's structure: to define a context, to define a
pattern or variable property, to state an open-ended knowledge structure
and indicate the unknowns and data access points, to explore a domain or
a range, etc. Or to state facts alongside the question, to indicate
expectation parameters of the answer(s). - 3. The setting of the
question is object(s) and relation(s). Associated objects and relations
can be explicit or implied, but does result in expectation parameters. -
4. The existential time frame or solidity or transitory frame cycle of
the question's objects and relations in regard to their setting is
another context involved in definitive consideration of answer
expectation parameters. - 5. - 6. . . . etc. There may be many more
foundational contexts that intersect in the formation and existence of
every question. Copyright 5/24/2005 Justin Coslor Question asking
systems Question -> Perception of meaning of question -> Search and
answer retrieval -> answer formulation -> interpretation of answer. In
short, QUESTION -> ANSWER(S).

The more methods of knowledge representation that are available to
model the perception of the meaning of the question, the more depth and
breadth the search scope will have in the answer retrieval process, and
the experimental data combining buffer will have more possibilities to
form experimental combination answers with. If the answers are
experimental, then they may need to be tested or proven valid. Not all
valid answers are useful though, and not all questions can be modeled
accurately. Question-Answer systems and Question asking systems are

subject to priority systems, in their exploration of patterns in contexts. Every question or series of questions is a rough draft of the question that will produce or point to the desired answer that contains the right level of detail of suitable content. Copyright 5/10/2005 Justin Coslor Re-defining basic question thought-forms: Why? = Is there a reason for how this came to be, and what is it? What? = The existence of this shall be called by a name that needs to be defined, and we are inquiring about that. When? = This occurred or shall occur at what time and day? How? = By what process does this function? Notice that I had to use "what" in every one of these (except I tried not to use "what" in it's own definition, which was difficult). Therefore "what" is the most important thought form to focus on. "What" is the algebraic domain of the relation "that", or "this", or "these", or "those"; and the range is unknown, and is entirely unbounded. "That", is a pointer to a specific instance of something in existence (whether it be in physical or Platonic reality). The difference between Platonic objects and physical objects is that Platonic objects are just pointers to other pointers, whereas physical objects are pointers that point to themselves in a loop. Physical objects can bound and/or link (like a chain) other physical objects because if we geometrize the representation of the pointers we have physics, since the pointers loop. We exist partially in physical reality, and partially in Platonic reality since we can make conversions between the two. It's like the difference between particles and waves... Copyright 5/11/2005 Justin Coslor Writing Tips

When I want to write, to figure out what to write I try to figure out a priority system, where I aim to invent the most important new idea that I'm either interested in (topically) or that is very important but that is only interesting enough to write down for somebody else to explore. Once I've focused on a topic I start asking questions and map it out and associate it to other areas and build networks of questions and answers and arbitrary data.

I have to feel like writing and be relaxed and well hydrated (slightly caffeinated helps), and it's best when I'm thinking at my best (not bogged down by emotions) I don't consider this entry an "idea" since I feel awful and am terribly lonely and depressed and have heartburn at the moment. I write best when I'm either really really happy (a bipolar high), or really really depressed (a bipolar low). 10/20/2004 Justin Coslor Regarding Education

If people could be taught first how to learn on their own, and next how to find and update their sources of information and resources, and then be taught creative and consistent logic and how to interact in their chosen forums of discourse, along with some skills as to how they can negotiate their insights and nurtured talents for wellbeing and non-harmful prosperity to an extent limited to what they can successfully and comfortably manage without bloating into the arena of greed or ill- intent; then they would have a great potential for doing a lot of good in the world and in the happiness of their daily lives. Lives lived purposefully. 10/28/2004 Justin Coslor It's important to be semi-autonomous rather than being just another domino. Copyright 6/1/2005 Justin Coslor Choice

Choice depends on having recognized options to choose from. The availability of options depends on a system of awareness, and the explorative mapping of solution spaces and/or experimentally created generation. Also an evaluation system or metric is necessary for the selection process to pick a suitable option. The initiation of choice can be voluntary or forced; and it can be activated out of necessity, or independently. Copyright 5/31/2005 Justin Coslor Creativity

Creative processes start out with a chosen medium, and then a random process is activated that generates a lot of possibilities, then it is a matter of choosing the best or most desirable possibilities and elaborating on them and linking them. That is what creativity means to me. The creator may also have several goals or requirements in mind, and be aware of juggling prerequisites. Copyright 5/28/2005 Justin Coslor
Intuitions
    Intuitions are sequences of inspiration, and are part possibility thinking, part logical thinking, and part random chance phenomenon. Intuitive truth requires proof. Copyright 8/13/2005 Justin Coslor Ideas and Probabilities
    Ideas change probabilities, and ideas come from experimentation: search, sort, and shuffle (grouping and storing patterns in contexts). Ideas guide courses of action and affect expectations, of which reactions are based on, and those are some of the probabilities ideas can change, but they can also pave the way for new systems and developments.
    Intentions guide experimentation, and logic guides methodology. Axioms define logic and modes of proof. Innate programming (instinct) and use of methodology in real-time guides intentions.
    Useful ideas change contexts dramatically, and in doing so, many of the patterns in those contexts are able to form lots of new associations and possibilities. The most sweeping ideas are at the axiom level, and as new axioms are added, contexts expand and develop greater depth and greater interconnectivity.

Book III:
Math Ideas:

Copyright 9/13/2004 Justin Coslor
Infinity
    Something that is infinite in one context may be finite in another context. For the re-definition of "infinite" is something that goes on forever along the dimensional framework of a given context. But once new axioms are applied to the context where that something went on forever, the context is changed, and thus so the definition of many if not all things that existed in the former context, and in many cases infinite objects may become quitet definable (finite).
------------------------------- 3/2/2005 update by Justin Coslor
Also, it's important to not that perspectives changes (such as recontexualizations), may come with different axiom sets than the original context. 10/19/2004 Justin Coslor Public Domain, free for well intended use only. The upper limits of NP-Completeness Polynomial time computations' upper limit can be described by saying "infinity^x", and that has finitely many dimensions of context, but infinite scope along those dimensions. Non-polynomial time computations can be described by "x^infinity", and that has finite scope, but infinitely many dimensions of context. As you can see, cannot exactly equal np, however, it can approximate an incomplete abstract summary of some parts of np, using part of p's scope. This is because exponents stand for the number of perpendicular or symmetrical dimensions that the variable exists in. So saying that p=np is like trying to say that infinity^x=x^infinity, which it clearly is not; but p can be composed of a selection of np's dimensions, as long as they have a common base for forming selective perspective. Copyright 10/17/2004 Justin Coslor Qualifying & Quantifying Dimensionality In equations such as $AnX^n + A\{n-1\}X^{n-1} + \ldots + A1X + A0 = 0$, the coefficients (An to A1) can be considered to be quantifiers,

and X^n to X or Y's etc, can be considered to be qualitative variables.
When the variables X, Y, etc have exponents or are multiplied
together, each combination of exponents and variables defines the
dimensionality of the planes that the equation is holding in relation to
one another, and the coefficients define the size or length or quantity
or magnitude of each dimensional/qualitative structure in the equation
that is held in relation to each other dimensional/qualitative structure
in the equation. Now some dimensional structures are best described by
equations that have more than two sides to the equal sign, such as those
that exist on higher prime and prime composite levels of balance than
most of current mathematics is based on. So we can only approximate
descriptions of those structures in a duality format if at all.
I guess a computer array or database or arrays of arrays can be used
to depict higher dimensionality, but past a certain number of dimensions
it surpasses the human brain's neuro- hardware's ability to visualize
the relations and dimensional complexity. Arrays can be used to list out
infinitely many dimensions categorically and quantitatively. However,
nobody as of yet has discovered a way to think of a way to bound the
classification of objects or situations using more than two extremes,
using dualities such as maximum and minimum to balance an equation.
Triality, or quintality, etc, along the prime numbers may indeed be
possible, though our brains don't seem to interpret the universe along
those dimensions as of yet. Perhaps eventually we will learn to adapt
higher logical foundations. Copyright 10/4/2004 Justin Coslor Spirals
(See the photos of the pictures depicted by this text on this date.) A
number that has exponents contains one perpendicular or symmetrical
dimension per exponent , so f^5 in this equation might look something
like the multidimensional picture of a spiral within a spiral within a
spiral within a spiral within a spiral. This is how my math invention
"Sine Spiral Graphing" applies to the discovery I made about
dimensionality (see journal entry dated 7/10/2004 Justin Coslor). The
line going through the center of the spiral might actually be a spiral,
a circle, an elliptical loop, a curve, or some combination of those.
This kind of visual notation ("Exponential Sine Spiral Graphing" I call
it) can be used in conjunction with conical orbit graphing I call it)
can be used in conjuntion with conical orbit graphing to simplify the
interaction visualizations of multiple spinning and/or orbiting bodies
that have at least one plane of rotation in common.
---------------------------- Update: Copyright 2/10/2005 Justin Coslor
The optimal structure of nanotechnology parallel-processing
supercomputer memory structure could be something like this f^5
composite exponential spiral, except with ribbons of memory units and
have vertical pipelines interconnecting each exponential layer of the
composite spiral, and have a brick made out of short columns of these
f^4 or f^5 or f^n spirals that are laterally connected on the ends of
each column and stack multiple columns on top of each other in sheets of
intensely interconnected spirals, like slices of a tree trunk. 7/10/2004
by Justin Coslor Light Spirals
For several weeks now I have believed that light (and other
emissions of convecting energy) particles/packets/quanta travel not in
waves, but in spirals and flocks of spirals. I came to this conclusion
after figuring out how to visualize Balmer's frequency equation (the one
with the Rydberg constant and electron shell radiuses: $f=R(1/Nf^2 -
1/Ni^2)$ where Nf is the outermost shell and Ni is the initial shell) in
terms of sine-spiral graphing (Sine-spiral graphing is something of my
own invention, and is a 3D resentation of circular motion, where the
sine-waves or cosine waves represented for all points in time as a

spiral (cosine of a point is X, sine at that point is Y, and time at that point is Z in the 3D coordinate system....remember the unit circle?) through time (or through a 3rd dimension if time is irrelevant or instantaneous or if motion is uniform)). See pg 67 of the comic book "Introducing Quantum Theory" by J.P. McEvoy and Oscar Zarate - Copyright 1996 (2003 reprint) ISBN: 1840460571 for Balmer's frequency equation. *Note: Waveforms only look like that from a perpendicular side-view, and I think this because, interestingly enough, 3D spirals look exactly like that when they are looked at from a perpendicular side view, which essentially is a 2D perspective. That is part of the basis of my sine-spiral graphing methods (I came up with the math for it when I got way behind in 10th grade Math-Analysis class). 7/11/2004 update by Justin Coslor Light Spirals Continued

To visualize it I juggled the equation around a little, and figured out the intent that went into creating the algorithm. In Nf^2 and Ni^2, f^2 and i^2 just means that the variable f exists in a two- dimensional plane where one f axis is perpendicular or symmetrical to every other variable in the composite of the multiplicative parts; and when numbers or values get plugged into those variables, the visualization depicts a specific graph within the context of that combined dimensionality. That is why multiplication is used in algorithms to combine variables that are proportional to each other. *Multiplication shows that they have a proportional relationship. **Multiplication can also show that variables' dimensionality can share the same space, by perceiving of them in the broader context of their dimensions' combined contexts (whether it be symbolic, semantic, algebraic, or geometrical). ***One variable=1 dimensional representation. Two variables=2 dimensional representation. Three variables=3D . . . There is a limit to our neuro hardware's dimensional ability. ****If a variable is squared it exists within a two-dimensional context, if it is cubed, it exists within a 3D context, etc. Copyright 5/6/1997 Justin Coslor Sine Spiral Graphing

A new method of graphing motion called "Sine Spiral Graphing" was developed by me when I was 16. It allows for simultaneously graphing the sine and cosine curves of an object in motion, three-dimensionally. Sine and cosine, when graphed simultaneously in two dimensions, look like two staggered intersecting waves traveling in the same general direction. (Fig. 1) There has been a need for developing better methods of graphing an object's two-dimensional (flat) motion through space over a period of time that more clearly shows the progression of travel. At present, mapping three-dimensional motion using different variables is more complicated, but could be a further application of the principles presented in the "Sine Spiral Graphing" method. The "Sine Spiral" is based on the spiral shape of two-dimensional circular motion graphed in three dimensions using this new graphing technique. The name is derived from the general name of the sine wave combined with what the actual 3D graph looks like: a spiral. This technique could be helpful for scientists and students alike in many applications. Some possible application for the Sine Spiral could be: - Plotting the motion of a bead in a hula hoop as it spins around one's waist. - Calculating the position of various atomic/subatomic particles moving in relation to each other over time. - Plotting the velocity and position of a point on an automobile wheel as sit spins down a runway or curvy hilly road. - Plotting the motion of a baseball spinning through the air as it travels forward to the catcher over a period of time. - Calculating the motion of a point on a bowling ball as it rolls down the lane over time. - Calculating the speeds and positions of a set of points, on various gears at work, in a clock in relation to each other over time. -

Calculating the motion of a point on a rocket ship, or of a point on a space satellite as it orbits a planet. - Plotting the movement of a chicken in a tornado.

All of these examples listed present graphing difficulties when depicted on a normal graph. The motions in these examples could be calculated on a computer and represented in a simulated fashion to show the actual movement in space for one point in time at a time. Concurrent Sine Spiral graphs can also be drawn for comparison of points on multiple moving objects. However, it would be difficult to graphically represent these motions for all points in time all at once. A simulation could be like a video, where one can only view one place on the video at a time. Viewing forward and reverse at the same time is not logistically possible on a video. However, when motion is three-dimensionally graphed on a computer using a Sine Spiral, it is possible to view these motions for all points in time all at once. A very effective way to manipulate and browse three-dimensional graphs (such as a Sine Spiral) on a computer is with Virtual Reality equipment. With Virtual Reality equipment, the perspective of the viewer can freely move around in space (on the graph) and see the 3D objects in one's graph from any perspective. In a Virtual Reality graph, the user can have total control over what is viewed and how it is viewed.

Understanding the trigonometric functions of sine, cosine, tangent, and their inverse counterparts is a necessity for understanding Sine Spiral Graphing. Trigonometric functions of real numbers, called "Circular Functions" (or Wrapping Functions), can be defined in terms of the coordinates of points on the unit circle with the equation $x^2+y^2=1$ having its center at the origin and a radius of 1. (Fig. 2)

There are three elements in a two-dimensional trigonometric function: the angle of rotation (sigma), the radius of the rotation r, and the (x,y) position of the point at that angle and radius. As can be seen in Figure 3, the x and y portions of the graph are always perpendicular to each other. Thus a right triangle is formed between the x, y, and radius sides. Right triangle rules can therefore be applied to this point in space (Brown/Robbins 190).

Such trigonometric functions as sine and cosine can be applied to the triangle formed by rotation. These functions, sin and cos, are of fundamental importance in all branches of mathematics. One can use points other than those on the unit circle to find values of the sine and cosine functions. (Fig. 4) If a point Q has coordinates (x,y), and it is at angle sigma in reference to the origin, (cos sigma) = x/r and (sin sigma) = y/r. To obtain a rough sketch of a sine wave, plot the points (t, sin t) (Fig. 5), then draw a smooth curve through them, and extend the configuration to the right and left in periodic fashion. This gives the portion of the graph shown in Figure 5 (Swolowski 78).

A cosine can be graphed in the same fashion by simply shifting the graph 90 degrees to the right. (Fig. 6) An object's circular motion can be described by either a sine wave or a cosine graphed in the same fashion. Such a wave is composed of the object's radius of rotation and the vperiod (number of degrees in on cycle) per unit of time that it rotates. Seeing an object's sine and cosine graph simultaneously greatly helps in visualizing the object's motion analytically compared how it found in real life. Watching an animation of an object spinning is the same as seeing the x and y coordinates (cosine and sine) of the object for each frame of the animation, one frame at a time. This is because one could see a scale view of its whole two-dimensional motion over a period of time. Visualizing an object's true motion in nature from merely looking at a graph of its sine or cosine can be difficult to conceptualize. For this reason, the Sine Spiral may be an improvement in current co-linear graphing (Fig. 7).

Velocity over the period of one rotation on a sine curve can be measured by dividing the distance traveled in one rotation by the amount of time it takes to complete that one rotation. Velocity = change in distance/change in time + direction.

Any change in velocity (a change in time) will change the distance between peaks of the spiral. The whole Z-axis around which the spiral revolves represents time passed. When the velocity is constant, the distance from peak to peak in the spiral is constant or each distance from one peak to another peak is the same. (Fig. 6) Therefore, if the distance from one peak to another changes somewhere in the spiral, this indicates that the velocity has changed at that point in time.

Within the Sine Spiral, some of the variables that can change in the object's motion are velocity, radius of rotation, position of axis of revolution, and the scale upon which measurements are based. The shape of this spiral is an indication of any and all of these variables. The change in the shape of the spiral correlates to the change in one or more of these variables. (Fig. 7)

Webster's Third New International Dictionary defines a spiral as "A three-dimensional curve (as a helix) with one or more turns around and axis." In current circular motion, the sine of the angle of rotation provides a Y value (Sine=Y/Radius of Rotation), while the cosine of that same angle provides and X value (Cosine=X/Radius of Rotation). These X and Y values are all that is needed to draw the two-dimensional models of rotation known as the sine curve and the two- dimensional models of rotation known as the sine curve and cosine curve (or sine wave). To my knowledge it has not been thought possible to graph this same motion in three dimensions though, because one needs an X, Y, and Z coordinate in order to graph in 3D. There can be an X and Y coordinate by finding the sine and cosine of a unit circle. All that is needed is a Z coordinate to make the circular motion graphable in three dimensions.

That Z coordinate could be representable by time, or speed of rotation, or even the period of degrees it takes for one complete rotation. In a sine wave, the period is 360 degrees. Using the period of degrees in one rotation, one can find a constantly increasing Z coordinate by dividing the current number of degrees traveled by the period of degrees it takes to complete one rotation. In short, degrees/period. The period can be depicted by a set amount of time. Finding a ratio between something that can be used as a reference point (one second vs the number of degrees in one rotation) to one's current progress in that measurement scale (number of seconds that have passed vs number of degrees that have been traveled) determine where one is on the Z- axis.

By dividing one's progress by a predetermined scale of reference, a new dimension can be generated in which to plot on a graph in order to illustrate this in three-dimensional fashion. This new dimension can be called the "Z-axis". Now that there is an X, Y, and Z dimension available, a three-dimensional model of an object's progress through its path of circular motion is possible.

For 3D motion, one can draw three spirals over the same T axis and where two of the spirals intersect, plot a point. Connecting the dots between the points gives one a tri-spiral (a spiral or shape that represents 3D motion over time). One can continue plotting the points with several objects and where the tri-spirals intersect, the objects intersect. One can break down the tri-spiral to find out where the X, Y, and Z coordinates are in space and the time coordinates of the intersection.

To use the Sine Spiral to map the 3D motion throughout time, one could mark the spiral with tags (or color code it) that tell one when and how far down the Z-axis it travels. Then to graph several objects to compare their motions and positions to each other, one can have a computer draw lines of the same color of the Z-tag, linking all of the objects that intersect on the two planes like the ZX plane, or the ZY plane. That way, one could identify when objects like planets line up on a plane or intersect.

There is much to benefit from in being able to graph an object's progress at the same time as its position in space. One can see time from an outside perspective and also see how an object's motion, position, and speed relate to any point in time. In many circumstances, it may be very useful to finally be able to get to see the general shape of an object's travel through all points in time all at once. This new method of graphing circular motion in three dimensions is the "Sine Spiral".

The graph forms a regularly spaced spiral whose axis is a straight line equidistant from the perimeter of the spiral. Changing the radius of rotation around a center axis changes the radius of the spiral around the Z axis. Changing the center of rotation in two-dimensional space (X, Y coordinates) makes the Z axis of the sign spiral curve up, down, or to the sides when graphed (instead of the normal straight line Z-axis).

For instance, an air hockey puck pinning in place would have a regular sign spiral that represents a point on the puck's perimeter that is traveling in a circle. Now if the spinning puck were to be slid across an air hockey table, that same point (on the perimeter of the puck) would have an irregular sine spiral whose radius would be constant, but the Z-axis around which the graph spirals would instantaneously bend at a ninety degree angle.

A computer can easily generate this three-dimensional picture of an object "N" at point "T" in time if the speed of travel is irregular (or at the ratio of degrees traveled to the period of one complete rotation if the speed is constant). (Fig. 8)

Graphing any two-dimensional motion (motion that moves in any direction on a flat plane), or rotation in three-dimensions using time or progress as the third dimension allows one to look at time from an outside perspective. The Sine Spiral can be used to graph any such two-dimensional motion, or any number of combinations of such motion. It can be used to graph several objects moving around in 2D (flat) space on the same plane. The Sine Spiral can be used to graph an object which has a rotation within a rotation, and so on (Fig. 9). In this case, each next level of rotation is on an incrementally larger scale. To view some of the higher levels of rotation, one must graph the object's motion over a longer period of time. This concept can relate to complex motions of a longer period of time. This concept can relate to complex motions of a large scale found in, for example, the universe. Sine Spiral graphing can literally be used to graph the motion of every particle in perceivable universe for all points in observable time, simultaneously (by bending the Z-axis appropriately to accommodate changes is axis orientation). Using the Sine Spiral, graphing motion in the Z-axis, or time, requires one to employ a means to mark or reference the Sine Spiral in order to distinguish how deep down the Z-axis the motion has traveled.

Without a Sine Spiral, one can only pick three-dimensions to see on a graph for all points in those dimensions. One could have X, Y, and Z coordinates on a 3D graph all at once, but only for one point in time per graph. Or one could illustrate motion in any two dimensions for all points in time using the Sine Spiral. Here are some of the dimensions from which one can choose: X, Y, Z, and Time. One can have four or more dimensions on a graph by selecting 3 variables form out of the X, Y, Z, and Time, as well as any number of descriptive, qualitative, categorical, computational, or other quantitative dimensions. These kinds of dimensions may appeal/apply to one's senses and could be described in "real" dimensions such as the Z-axis and others.

With 3D applications using this concept (once improved methods of graphing 3D motion with the sine spirals are better developed), other more complex spirals can be mapped. Such 3D applications could include the universe in their motion through space throughout all time to see where certain ones meet or line up), and graphing the motion of particles of a sun during a supernova (the spiral would look similar to a tangent spiral as described below). The Sine Spiral may be an improvement in the graphing of nonlinear and linear motion. With the help of the recent Virtual Reality technology, most any computer can be used to build 3D models such as Sine Spirals. We can construct and view a Sine Spiral and have complete control over the graph, viewing it in 3D space as if it were physically here.

There are many new math applications and theorems that may apply to this concept. Different types of spirals are possible with the general Sine Spiral method. Such shapes could include the Sine Tube (a sine spiral whose period is infinitely small), the Tangent Spiral (which uses a sine spiral whose period is infinitely small), the Tangent Spiral (uses the equation Tan sigma = $(y/r)/ (x/r)$ for the x and y coordinates), and the secant spiral (uses sec sigma = $1/(x/r)$ for the coordinate and csc sigma = $1/(y/r)$ for the y coordinate). Also, in either two-dimensional or three-dimensional motion (when a graphing method is available), an object can be spinning in a circle within a circle (each level of rotation incrementally bigger than the previous), and this will make a very special type of Sine Spiral that looks like a spiral within a spiral within a spiral, etc., depending on how many levels of rotation are going on. More new math applications ar sure to be found that can apply to the Sine Spiral as it is used.

Graphing three-dimensional motion with the Sine Spiral is more difficult to do, but can be done effectively. Graphing three-dimensional motion using the Sine Spiral needs further refinement at this time, but will hopefully be available for use in the near future. There are many new avenues that open up as people figure things out in science and math. The Sine Spiral may be another door in mathematics ready to be opened up and entered. Through this door may be a whole new way to look at things, a way to see objects in nonlinear motion from a standpoint outside of time. ------------------------------ Works Cited: Brown R., and D. Robbins, "Advanced Mathematics: A Precalculus Course"

Boston: Houghton Mifflin Company 1987. Fleenor C., M. Shanks, and C. Brumfiel. "The Elementary Functions".

Boston: Addison-Wesley Publishing Company, 1973. Gove, P.B., ed. "Webster's Third New International Dictionary, Unabridged".

Springfield, MA: Miriam-Webster, 1986. Manougian, M.N. "Trigonometry with Applications".

Tampa, FL: Mariner Publishing Co., 1980. Swokowski, E.W. "Fundamentals of Trigonometry".

Boston: Prindle, Weber & Schmidt, Incorporated, 1982.

------------------------------ Copyright 6/28/2003 Justin Coslor Conical Satellite Orbit Graphing (See Diagrams dated 10/4/2004, 3/1/2004, and 9/15/2001)

I do think the conical satellite orbit graphing idea I thought of in winter 2001 (or the year before) could still be something valuable in detecting and calculating collisions and for 3D space junk detection. It's based on the hypothesis that if you compress a half-sphere into the shape of a cone, the 180 degree arcs become straight lines, and straight lines are easier to represent, interpret depth of, and run calculations on than arcs. Elliptical orbits would just re straight lines at an angle, each line representing the orbital path of an object in space. Where two or more lines intersect, a collision is possible at the point by either accelerating or de-accelerating the objects that the lines represent.

Each object in a hemisphere cone is represented by a maximum and minimum altitude, and an angle representing the direction in which the object is traveling. There is one cone for each hemisphere. The neat thing about the conical format is that you can see how a bunch of objects, traveling in different directions at various altitudes, stack up along a common line of altitude protruding through the center of the planet, sun, moon, atom, galaxy, etc, and you can see how this line of altitude intersects each of those objects at two points in time (one for each hypersphere cone), along their various paths of travel.

Conical orbit graphing is a way to group a set of satellites (or other objects in orbit) by a single line protruding through the center of the central mass out into space (with a longitude and latitude coordinate for each hemisphere from which the line emerges). All sorts of nifty computer software functions can be incorporated into this as well, such as having a 2D map of the central mass (such as a planetary map or electron orbital map) as a clickable image map that generates a unique pair of orbit cones for each coordinate (one for each hemisphere of the hypersphere for objects traveling 360 degrees or more around the planet). It would have a timing component as well and can be used as a multi-body gravitational clock, viewable with virtual reality equipment or a regular computer. There can also be a range component that highlights any possible collisions within a certain proximity of the satellites in focus (the satellites that intersect a common axis of altitude, have one pair of cones for each axis of altitude). The user should also be able to zoom in and out, rotate the cones, focus on different axis' of altitude, combine complex orbits with sine- spiral graphing techniques (see my paper on that), and watch the satellites travel along their path lines in real-time (at an adjustable rate) using live or recorded data collected from sensors and observational equipment. It would help if most modern satellites were equipped to detect space junk and satellites around them and relay it back to the ground so that the world has a constantly updated fairly accurate map of all of the objects and space junk in orbit around the earth, since space flight has been compared to flying through a high-speed shooting gallery. Ideally, some kind of Star Trek-like/Tesla Wardencliffe-tower-like shields or something are needed for the safety of that hazard (but not for use as a weapon), but a good 3D navigational map can't hurt. For each satellite the computer can run a conical orbit graphing collision detection test for each point in time along it's projected path of travel.

The main use of conical orbit graphing as I see it, is for detecting collisions at points along a line of altitude, using one pair of cones for each point in time (or as a 3D interactive video). The user should be able to pick a time and x-y coordinate, see the satellites that intersect that line of altitude, then zoom in on the part of the path of the satellite that they are interested in, then click on a point in that path, and a new set of cones will be generated using that point as an altitude line in the center of the cones so that you can then see what possible collisions and path intersections there are for that point in the satellite flight path-time. All as straight lines so that it's easier to comprehend in complex situations. The computer calculations might even be quicker than calculating arcs. I'd assume elliptical arcs to be the most computationally intensive using traditional methods, but they too could probably be represented as straight lines in the software (going diagonally across the cones from one height to another height, and then the opposite for the other cone). It would be a 3D software tool for visualization and collision-interception calculation (and might be able to help protect all countries from incoming intercontinental thermonuclear ballistic missiles by combing this visualization method with a ground-based or space-based or airplane-based or reusable non-offensive missile based laser/maser anti-ballistic missile defense system. There might be many other beneficial uses for this visualization method that I haven't thought of yet (such as charting asteroids around Saturn or something; though hopefully it won't ever be used for, or even be useful for offensive purposes of any kind).. I haven't written any of the code yet or figured out much of the math yet to make it possible yet. Scholarly help is encouraged. Copyright 8/28/2005 Justin Coslor Applications of Conical Hyperhemisphere Graphing When Combined With Sine Spiral Graphing (See my papers dated 5/6/1997 and 6/28/2003.)

A Sine Spiral graph can be used to depict how an object rotates in N dimensions as it moves from point to point in time (as though it were rotating in place through time without actually traveling forward along a path). Then those time coordinates can be linked to a conical orbit graph of the distance vectors that the object moves through along its path (or use a 3D Cartesian Coordinate grid of its path if it isn't going to travel a full orbit around the planet...or not...). This combination of graphing techniques works regardless of whether the object is below, on, or above the surface of the Earth, or other center of mass in space. For instance it could be used for mapping the path of a vessel that goes from under the ocean, up into the sky, and out into space into an orbit around the moon or something. ***************** Each layer of the hyperhemisphere cone is a polar grid of a different altitude. Elliptical and circular orbits are represented as straight lines going across a pair of cones and intersect with an axis of altitude line that goes vertically through the center of each cone, where the axis of altitude represents a line going through the center of the planet and out both sides into space. Elliptical orbits go diagonally across the cones in this fashion from one altitude to another, and back the opposite way in the cone that represents the other half of the hyperhemisphere. Circular orbits go straight across the cones at whatever altitude and declination they happen to be on. *****************

Space stations could use these mapping techniques to coordinate their motion and to dock incoming spacecraft, and it could be useful for spaceship navigation and satellite positioning, coordination, and communication routing too. Navy submarines could use these sine spiral + conical hyperhemisphere (or sine spiral + Cartesian or polar) graphs when planning and plotting routes through the oceans of the world through different depths and complex courses. Air-Force planes in perpetual (or merely long distance) flight could also use it to plan or plot their courses, so could airlines. It could simplify autonomous agent motion through extremely complicated environments, such as space, or for nanobots navigation in a chip or in colloidal fluid, or autopiloted aircraft in extremely crowded skies (such as autopiloted personal aircraft for overcrowded cities). Cross Domain Relations, for the Mathematics of Alternative Route Exploration Aside from the first order logic stuff, the ideas and depictions in this paper were originally conceived of and are Copyright 5/22/2004 by Justin M. Coslor, ALL RIGHTS RESERVED (Please contact me for conditions of use...). This Rough Draft was typed on 6/9/2004 in AbiWord on an X86-Compatible Personal Computer running GNU Sarge (a free Debian Linux Operating System), and was encouraged by the FRDCSA.ORG project.

These ideas are intended to enhance the ability to discover and invent new routes in any field of study, and to aid in evaluating the relative utility of known routes, as well as to simplify some of the problems posed by computability theory.

Figure 1.

From the foundations of relational logic, we already know that: if a relation is xRy: X-->Y, then it is injective; or if xRy: X<-->Y, then it is bijective; or if xRy: X-->(y1, y2, ..., yp), then it is surjective; We also know that if a functional relation is xRy: y=f(x)=m where f(x) represents an arbitrary function of the domain X that yields a set of unique m's that are sub-ranges (y's) within the bounds of the range Y (a.k.a. the Class Y), where each m corresponds to a uniquely arbitrary domain x through the functional relation f(x). In this case, [f(x)]=R in the equation xRy. (*Remember for later that any mathematical operator (+, -, /, *, etc.) can be a relation. Any piece of computer software can also be treated as a relation, since software performs operations, and is basically a collection of algebraicly-tied operators.) But perhaps, we can broaden the scope of the Context in order to allow for more possibilities. This "broadening", may include metaphoric operations and metaphoric relations between the data type(s) of the functional relation(s) in focus and various specified number sets, orderings, and systems of numbers (including symbolic ones). (*We'll cover more on this later.) Let us introduce a new type of relation, that is a relation that relates relations, and let us call it a Cross-Domain Relation, and depict it as such: One goal of this paper is to show a system to accurately depict the following kinds of relation: xCy: (x1, x2, ..., xp)-->knEY (injective), or xCy: (x1, x2, ..., xp)<-->knEY (bijective), or xCy: (x1, x2, ..., xp)-->(k1, k2, ..., kn)EY (surjective); where every sub-range k that is an element of the range Y, has multiple domains that relate to each k in a unique way (through a unique route). Each sub-domain in the Domain X can come from different contexts and each sub- domain may operate under a different relation to specific sub-ranges in Y than other sub- domains relations to those same sub-ranges in Y. In these relations, some of the sub-domains may be injective, some may be bijective, and some may be surjective. In order to label and order each set of sub-domains that is part of a unique cross-domain relation, we introduce the ordering term "n". We can use the "n" component here to differentiate and/or order cross-domain relations, by combining the ordering of cross-domain-related sub-domains (i.e. nCx) with the individual relations between those sub-domains and any given sub-ranges (i.e. xRy), as such: nCx: N-->X (injective), or nCx: N<-->X (bijective), or nCx: N-->{x1, x2, ..., xp} (surjective), then nCxRy describes the cross-domain relation where n is an element in the cross-domain N such that x=f(n), and x is an element of a particular cross-domain subset n (as well as being a sub-domain of the domain X), where x has a relation (a.k.a. a route) to a particular sub-range y in Y.; (***Note: every x in X and/or every n in N can come from vastly different contexts, yet still lead to the same y(s) in Y.) where for

each sub-range y, f(n) is every function in the cross-domain N that
leads to multiple sub-domains in X that lead to the the multilateral
result k (which is a specific singular sub-range y in the Class Y with
multiple relations leading to it from the domain X) through the route:
F[C{f(x)}]-->kEY (kEY means k is an Element of Y), where C{f(x)}=n and
y=f(x) and x=f(n), and k represents any specific unique sub-range in Y
that can be arrived at via multiple domains' functional relations, where
each of the multiple domain's relations goes from any sub-domain x in X
to the same specific sub- range y in Y; where F[N] is the set of all
routes to all k's in Y, K is the set of all k's in Y, and F[n] is the a
relation describing set of all routes to a specific k in Y. k is used to
depict sub-ranges that have multiple ways to arrive at them; that is to
say, ways that include origin variations, and intermediary relation
combinations (middle-man combinations). In short: "If some unique X's
yield some of the same unique y's through various relations, then those
X's are said to have "cross-domain relations", because those domains
have some relations whose end results have something in common."
^^^^^^^^^^^^^^^^^^This is what I was trying to draw and put into an
equation format. I'm not sure if I succeeded, but probably. It seemed
like there needed to be a formal word for what I was trying to depict as
relations that relate different contexts' functions' domains by a
representable equivalence or similarity in their ranges (when there is
exists such a representable equivalence or similarity), so that's how I
came up with the name "cross- domain relations". Computer software can
essentially be treated as such functions, for which cross-domain
relations that lead to alternative routes may exist for any given set or
class of software functions. It's basically all about alternative
routes. Such a mapping can be quite useful for exploring alternative, or
previously unconsidered, or unknown possibilities and modalities. In
Figure 1., X is a class that contains domains that lead to ranges within
the class Y. There may be other classes that lead to those ranges, even
if they do so indirectly through other classes by broadening the
applicable context. By saying "lead to them" I mean "relate to them" in
any "chosen" way(s). The route equations can get very complex the more
classes and destinations you're analyzing when looking for and mapping
cross-domain relations. In practice, the user ends up with a concise
pack of cross-domain relation equations that summarizes the entire
complexity of the known patterns in the contexts of any situation or
model. The equation packs can also be used to represent the possible
outlets to explore for new patterns based on perceived priority of their
beginning class of categories, and perceived
attainability/computability. . . mark off potentially infinite patterns
and recursive loops accordingly, after exploring the first few layers
only. Conclusion: Cross-domain relations can be used when depicting,
predicting, finding, manipulating, creating, using, analyzing,
backtracking, tracing, comparing, and reverse engineering alternative
routes to anything, in any field of application.

Examples: (*In the following examples I have defined the "underscore"
character "_" to be the equivalent of the logical statement "OR", which
is equivalent of the English language statement "and/or". I use the "_"
character to link multiple routes to a sub-range, so that the patterns
of the context of that sub-range can all be packaged into one continuous
string. Such a string can then be parsed easily and sorted according to

factors such as: route-scale (number of computable degrees or nodes v.s.
potentially infinite possibilities), route category, route-size, relative
route location, etc.)
Example 1:
     In Figure 1., the domain x2 has an alternative route to y1 through
the cross-domain relation n1Cx2Ry1_n1Cx1Cy1 where n1Cx2Ry1=Route k1, and
n1Cx1Cy1=Route k2. ((In my examples I like to use C to represent
bijective relations, and R to represent surjective or injective
relations.) *Note that x1Cy1Cn1=n1Cx1Cy1) So in this example k1 and k2
are the known routes to y1, and since we know about more than one route
to y1, we can call k1 and k2 cross-domain relations. Or we can simply
reference that group of routes by the meta-name k1_k2.
                                                            Figure 1.

     The following are Graph Theory Examples of Cross-Domain Relations:
(**In the following examples, I use R to represent an injective or
surjective route, and use C to represent the continuous directional flow
of a bijective route. I use the symbol "$" to indicate that the routes
on each side of the "$" have a bijective relationship. The "$" symbol is
used when comparing two or more routes. The "=>" symbol means "directly
implies".) Example 2: First have a look at Figure 2. (***Note: in ACB,
(a1Cb1)$(b1Ca1), because BCA exists.)
                                                            Figure 2.
Alternative routes to A from C:
ARC=a2Ra2 => a2 = ACCk1
ACBRC=a1Cb1Rb3_ a1Cb1Ca1Cb1Rb3 => ACCk2_ACCk3
ACBCDCC=a1Cb1Cb2Cd1Cd2_ABD$C=a1b2d2 => Routes ACCk4 through
ACCk11
     (****Many more complex routes beginning at A and terminating at C
exist, and can be very explicitly depicted in this manner.)

     Example 3: In Figure 2, by entering each line's node relationship
into a computer in a format such as: [ACB,BCD,DCC,BRC,ARC,ARF,FCE,FCC],
(<----This is the Context.) (Next I'll describe the Patterns in that
Context...) the computer can generate on the fly all of the possible
routes from any given node to any other given node, including curtailed
potentially infinite loop structures (by representing loop structures
via the "$" operator, as noted earlier), and it can explicitly represent
the optimal routes and rank the suboptimal routes using relation and
cross-domain relation notation. Perhaps in some situations, one might
even order the routes by largest perimeter of closed polygonal circuit
region to smallest polygonal circuit perimeter, followed by largest open
leg to smallest open leg, when declaring a context. (*****Where ";" is
the character that indicates the parsing of each closed-circuit
polygonal region or open leg in this notation variation.) This might
look something like: [ARC_CCF_ARF;ARC_ACB_BRC;BCD_DCC_BRC;FCE] ...if the
proportions were correctly represented in my diagram, that is...
                                                            Figure 2.
     Hierarchical Number Theory: Graph Theory Conversions Looking for
patterns in this: Prime odd and even cardinality on the natural number
system (*See diagram). First I listed out the prime numbers all in a

row, separated by commas. Then above them I drew connecting arcs over top of every other odd prime (of the ordering of primes). Over top of those I drew an arc over every two of those arcs, sequentially. Then over top of every sequential pair of those arcs I drew another arc, and so on. Then I did the same thing below the listing of the numbers, but this time starting with every other even prime.

   Then I sequentially listed out whole lot of natural numbers and did the same thing to them down below them, except I put both every other even and every other odd hierarchical ordering of arcs over top of one another, down below the listing of the natural number system.

   Then over top of the that listing of the natural number system I transposed the hierarchical arc structures from the prime number system; putting both every other even prime and every other odd prime hierarchically on top of each other, as I previously described. *Now I must note that in all of these, in the center of every arc I drew a line going straight up or down to the center number for that arc. (See diagram.)

   In another example, I took the data, and spread out the numbers all over the page in an optimal layout, where no no hierarchical lines cross each other, but the numbers act as nodal terminals where the hierarchical arches sprout out of. (See Diagram) This made a very beautiful picture which was very similar to a hypercube that has been unfolded onto a 2D surface. Graph Theory might be able to be applied to hierarchical representations that have been re-aligned in this manner, and in that way axioms from Graph Theory might be able to be translated into Hierarchical Number Theory.

   The center-poles are very significant because when I transposed the prime number structures onto the natural number system there is a central non-prime even natural number in the very center directly between the center-poles of the sequential arc structures of the every other even prime and every other odd prime of the same hierarchical level and group number. The incredibly amazing thing is that when dealing with very large prime numbers, those prime numbers can be further reduced by representing them as an offset equation of the central number plus or minus an offset number. The beauty of is, that the since the central numbers aren't prime, they can be reduced in parallel as the composite of some prime numbers, that when multiplied together total that central number; and those prime composite numbers can be further reduced in parallel by representing each one as their central number (just like I previously described) plus or minus some offset number, and so on and so on until you are dealing with very managably small numbers in a massively parallel computation. The offset numbers can be similarly crunched down to practically nothing as well. This very well may solve a large class of N-P completeness problems!!! Hurray! It could be extremely valuable in encryption, decryption, heuristics, pattern recognition, random number testing, testing for primality in the search for new primes, several branches of mathematics and other hard sciences can benefit from it as well. I discovered pretty much independently, just playing around with numbers in a coffee shop one day on 1/31/2005, and elaborated on 2/1/2005, and it was on 2/4/2005 when describing it to a friend who wishes to remain anonymous that I realized this nifty prime-number crunching technique, a few days after talking with the Carnegie Mellon University Logic and Computation Grad Student Seth Casana, actually it was then that I realized that prime numbers could be represented as an offset equation, and then I figured out how to reduce the offset equations to sets of smaller and smaller offset equations. I was showing Seth the diagrams I had drawn and the patterns in them. He commented that it looked like a Friege lattice or something. I think After I pointed out the existance of central numbers in the diagrams Seth told me that sometimes people represent prime numbers as an offset, and that all he could think of was that they could be some kind of offset or something. He's a total genius. He's graduating this year with a thesis on complexity theory and the philosophy of science. He made a bunch of Flash animations that teach people epistemology. Copyright 2/1/2005 Justin Coslor Rough draft typed 3/19/2005. This is an entirely new way to perceive of number systems. It's a way to perceive of them hierarchically. Many mathematical patterns may ready become apparent for number theorists as larger and larger maps in this format are drawn and computed. Hopefully some will be in the prime number system, as perceived through a variety of other numbering systems and forms of cardinality. (See photos.) Copyright 3/25/2004 Justin Coslor Hierarchical Number Theory Applied to Graph Theory

When every-other-number numerical hierarchies are converted into dependency charts and then those dependency charts are generalized and pattern matched to graphs and partial graphs of problems, number theory can apply to those problems because the hierarchies are based on the number line of various cardinalities.

I had fun at Go Club yesterday, and while I was at the gym I thought of another math invention. It was great. I figured out how to convert a graph into a numerical hierarchy which is based on the number line, so number theory can apply to the graph, and do so by pattern matching the graph to the various graphs that are generated by converting numerical hierarchical representations of the number line into dependency charts. I don't know if that will make sense without seeing the diagrams, but it's something like that. The exciting part is that almost any thing, concept, game, or situation can be represented as a graph, and now, a bunch of patterns can be translated into being able to apply to them. Copyright 1/31/2005 Justin Coslor Odd and Even Prime Cardinality First twenty primes: 2, 3, 5, 7, 11, 13, 17, 19, 23, 29, 37, 41, 43, 47, 53, 59, 61, 67, 71, 73. ------------------- *See the photo of the digram I drew on the original page. What properties and relations are there between the odd primes? First ten odd primes: 2, 5, 11, 17, 23, 37, 43, 53, 61, 71. First five odd odd primes: 2, 11, 23, 43, 61. First five odd even primes: 5, 17, 37, 53, 71. First ten even primes: 3, 7, 13, 19, 29, 41, 47, 59, 67, 73. First five even even primes: 7, 19, 41, 59, 73. First five even odd primes: 3, 13, 29, 47, 67.
----------------------- $prime^{(odd^4)} = prime^{(odd)^{(odd)^{(odd)^{(odd)}}}}$ = 2, 61, . . $prime^{(odd^3)} = prime^{(odd)^{(odd)^{(odd)}}}$ = 2, 23, 43, 61, . . . $prime^{(odd^2)} = prime^{(odd)^{(odd)}}$ = 2, 11, 23, 43, 61, . . . $prime^{(odd)} = prime^{(odd)}$ = 2, 5, 11, 17, 23, 37, 43, 53, 61, 71, . . . $prime^{(odd)^{(even)}}$ = 5, 17, 37, 53, 71, . . . $prime^{(even)^{(odd)}}$ = 3, 13, 29, 47, 67, . . . ------------------------------- Copyright 6/10/2005 Justin Coslor HOPS: Hierarchical Offset Prefixes

For counting hierarchically, prefix each set by the following variables: parity, level, and group (group starting number). Then use that group starting number as the starting position, and count up to the number from zero placed at that starting position for representation of a number prior to HOP computation. I need to develop a calculation method for that representation.

Have a high-level index which lists all of the group starting numbers for one of the highest rows, then the rest of the number's group numbers can be derived for any given level above or below it. All calculations should access this index.

If I was to look for the pattern "55" in a string of numbers, for example, I might search linearly and copy all two-digit locations that start with a "5" into a file, along with the memory address of each, then throw out all instances that don't contain a "5" as the second digit. That's one common way to search. But for addresses with a log of digits, such as extremely large numbers, this is impractical and it's much easier to do hierarchical level math to check for matches. The simplest way to do it is a hierarchical parity check + level check + group # check before proceeding to check both parities of every subgroup on level 1 of that the offset number. The offset begins at zero at the end of the prefix's group number, and a micro-hierarchy is built out of that offset. For large numbers, this is much faster than using big numbers for everything. Example: Imagine the number 123,456,789 on the number line. We'll call it "N". N = 9 digits in decimal, and many more digits in binary. In HOP notation, N = parity.level.group.offset. If I had a comprehensive index of all the group numbers for a bunch of the levels I could generate a prefix for this # N, and then I'd only have to work with a tiny number that is the difference between the closest highest group and the original number, because chances are the numbers I apply it to are also offset by that prefix or a nearby prefix. The great part about hierarchical offset prefixes is that it makes every number very close to every other number because you just have to jump around from level to level (vertically) and by group to group (horizontally).

I'll need to ask a programmer to make me a program that generates an index of group numbers on each level, and the program should also be able to do conversions between decimal numbers and hierarchical offset prefixes (HOPs). That way there are only four simple equations necessary to add, subtract, multiply, divide any two HOP numbers: just perform the proper conversions between the HOPs' parity, levels, groups, and offsets.

Parity conversions are simple, level conversions are just dealing with powers of 2, group conversions are just multiples of 2 + 1, and offset conversions just deal with regular mathematics using small numbers. Copyright 7/7/2005 Justin Coslor Prime Breakdown Lookup Tables

Make a lookup table of all of the prime numbers in level 1 level.group.offset notation, and calculate values for N levels up from there for each prime in that same level.group.offset notation using the level 1 database. 2^n = distance between prime $2^{(n + m)}$ and prime $2^{(n + (m + 1))}$.

Center numbers are generated by picking another prime on that same level somehow (I'm not positive how yet), and the number in-between them is the center number. Center number factoring can be done repeatedly so that, for example, if you wanted to multiply a million digit number by a million digit number, you could spread that out into several thousand small number calculations, and in that way primes can be factored using center numbers + their offsets.

Also, prime number divisor checking can be done laterally in parallel by representing each divisor in level.group.offset notation and then converting the computation into a set of parallel processed center number prime breakdown calculations, which would be significantly faster than doing traditional divisor checking, especially for very large divisors, assuming you have a parallel processor computer at your disposal, or do distributed computing, and do multiprocessing/multi-threading on each processor as well. Copyright 10/7/2004 Justin Coslor Prime divisor-checking in parallel processing pattern search. *I assume that people have always known this information. Prime Numbers are not: 1. Even --> Add all even numbers to the reject filter. 2. Divisible by

other prime numbers --> Try dividing all numbers on the potentially
prime list by all known primes. 3. Multiples of other prime numbers -->
Parallel process: Map out in parallel multiples of known primes up to a
certain range for the scope of the search field, and add those to the
reject filter for that search scope. When you try to divide numbers on
the potentially prime list, all of those divisions can be done in
parallel where each prime divisor is granted its own process, and
multiple numbers on the potentially prime list for that search scope
(actually all of the potentials) could be divisor-checked in parallel,
where every number on the potentially prime list is granted its own
complete set off parallel processes, where each set contains a separate
parallel process for every known prime. So for less than half of the
numbers in the search scope will initially qualify to make it onto the
potentially prime list for divisor checking. And all of the potentially
prime numbers will need to have their divisor check processes augmented
as more primes are discovered in the search scope. The Sieve of
Eratosthenes says that the search scope is in the range of n^2, where n
is the largest known prime. Multiple search scopes can be running
concurrently as well, and smaller divisor checks will always finish much
sooner than the larger ones (sequentially) for all numbers not already
filtered out. 12/24/2004 Justin Coslor Look for Ways to Merge Prime
Number Perception Algorithms I don't yet understand how the Riemann Zeta
Function works, but it might be compatible with some of the mathematics
I came up with for prime numbers (sequential prime number word list
heuristics, active filtering techniques, and every other number
groupings on the primes and on the natural number system). Maybe there
are lots of other prime number perception algorithms that can also be
used in conjunction with my algorithms. ??? -------------- Try applying
my algorithm for greatly simplifying the representation of large prime
numbers to the Riemann Zeta function. My algorithm reduces the
complexity of the patterns between sequential prime numbers to a fixed
five variable word for each pair of sequential primes, and there are
only 81 possible words in all. So as a result of fixing the pattern
representation language to only look for certain qualities that are in
every sequential prime relationship, rather than having infinite
possibilities and not knowing what to look for, patterns will emerge
after not to long into the computer runtime. These patterns can then be
used to predict the range of the scope of future undiscovered prime
numbers, which simplifies the search for the next prime dramatically,
but even more important than that is that my algorithm reduces the
cardinality complexity (the representation) of each prime number
significantly for all primes past a certain point, so in essence, this
language I've invented is a whole new number system, but I'm not sure
how to run computations on it. . .though it can be used with a search
engine as a cataloging method for dealing with extremely large numbers.
My algorithm is in this format: The Nth prime (in relation to the prime
that came before it) = the prime number nearest to [the midpoint of the
Nth prime, whether it be in the upper half or the lower half] : in
relation to the remainder of that "near-midpoint-prime" when subtracted
from the Nth prime. The biggest part always gets listed to the left of
the smaller part (with a ratio sign separating them), and if for the N-
1th prime if the prime prime part got listed on one side and in the next
if it's on the opposite side we take note of that. Next we find the
difference in the two parts and note if it is positive or negative, even
or odd, and lastly we compare it to the N-1th difference to see if it is
up, down, the same, or if N-1's difference is greater than 1 and N's
difference is 1 then we say it has been "reset". If the difference jumps

from 1 to a larger difference in N's difference we say it's "undo
reset". Also, the difference is the absolute value of the
"near-midpoint-prime" minus the remaining amount between it and the Nth
prime. Now each of these qualities can be represented by one letter and
placed in one of four sequential places (categories) to make a four
character word. Numbers could even be used instead of characters, but
that might confuse people (though not computers). *******************
"Prime Sequence Matcher" (to be made into software) *******************
This whole method is Copyright 10/25/2004 Justin Coslor, or even sooner
(most likely 10/17/2004, since that's when it occurred to me. I thought
of this idea to help the whole world and therefore must copyright it to
ensure that nobody hordes or misuses it. The algorithms behind this
method that I have invented are free for academic use by all United
Nations member nations, for fair good intent only towards everyone.
------------------------------- Download a list of the first 10,000
prime numbers from the Internet, and consider formating it in EMACS to
look something like this: 12 23 35 47 5 11 6 13 . . . 10,000 ____ and
name that file primelist.txt ---------------------- Write a computer
program in C or Java called "PrimeSequenceMatcher" that generates a file
called "primerelations.txt" in the following format based on
calculations done on each of line of the file "primelist.txt".
primelist.txt->PrimeSequenceMatcher->primerelations.txt file:
primerelations.txt 2 3 2:1 diff 1 left, pos, odd, same 3 5 3:2 diff 1
left, pos, even, up 4 7 5:2 diff 3 left, pos, even, same 5 11 7:4 diff 3
LR, neg, even, down(or reset) 6 13 6:5 diff 1 right, pos, even, up(or
undo reset) 7 17 10:7 diff 3 . . . N __ __:__ diff __ For the C program
see pg. 241 to 251 of Kernigan and Ritchie's book, "The C Programming
Language", for functions that might be useful in the program. See the
scans of my journal entries from 10/17/2004, 10/18/2004, and 10/24/2004
for details on the process (*Note, there may be a few errors, and the
paperwork is sort of sloppy for those dates...), and turn it into an
efficient explicit algorithm. **2/22/2005 Update: I wrote out the gist
of the algorithms for the software in my 10/26/2004 journal entry. The
point of the generating the file primerelations.txt is to run the file
through pattern searching algorithms, and build a relational database,
because since the language of the primes's representation in my method
is severely limited, patterns might emerge. Nobody knows whether or not
the patterns will be consistent in predicting the range that the next
primes will be in, but I hope that they will, and it's worth doing the
experiment since that would be a remarkable tool to have discovered. The
patterns may reveal in some cases which is larger: the
nearest-to-midpoint prime or it's corresponding additive part. Where the
sum equals the prime. That would tell you a general range of where the
next prime isn't at. Also the patterns may in some cases have a
predictable "diff" value, which would be immensely valuable in knowing,
so that you can compare it to the values of the prime that came before
it, which would give a fairly close prediction of where the next prime
may lye. By looking at the pattern of the ordering of sentences, we can
possibly tell which side of the ratio sign the nearest-to-midpoint prime
of the next prime we are looking for lies on (and thus know whether it
is in the upper half or the lower half of the search scope). The search
scope for the next prime number is in the range of the largest known
prime squared. We might also be able to in some cases determine how far
from the absolute value of the difference between the nearest-to-
midpoint prime and the prime number we are looking for, that the prime
number that we are looking for is. Copyright 10/26/2004 to 10/27/2004
Justin Coslor I hereby release this idea under The GNU Public License

Agreement (GPL). *************************** Prime Sequence Matcher
Algorithm ************************** (This algorithm is to be turned into
software. See previous journal entries that are related.) Concept
conceived of originally on 10/17/2004 by Justin Coslor Trends in these
sequential prime relation sentences might emerge as lists of these
sentences are formed and parsed for all, or a large chunk of, the known
primes. ----------------------------- The following definitions are
important to know in order to understand the algorithm: nmp = the prime
number nearest to the midpoint of "the Nth prime we are representing
divided by 2" aptnmp = adjacent part of the nmp = prime number we are
representing minus nmp prime/2 = (nmp+aptnmp)/2 = the midpoint of the
prime nmp = (2 * midpoint) - aptnmp aptnmp = (2 * midpoint) - nmp prime
= 2 * midpoint We take notice of whether nmp is greater than, equal to,
or less than aptnmp. diff = |nmp - aptnmp| N prime = nmp:aptnmp or
aptnmp:nmp, diff = |nmp - aptnmp|

a	b	c	d
left	pos	even	up
right	neg	odd	down
LR	null		same
RL			reset
			undoreset

    Each possible word can be abbreviated as a symbolic character or
symbolic digit, so the sentence is shortened to the size of a four
character word or four digit number. *Note: "a" only = "same" when prime
= 2 (.....that is, when N = 1) **Note: If "c" ever = "same", then N is
not prime, so halt. "abcd" has less than or equal to 100 possible
sequential prime relation sentences (SPRS)'s, since the representation
is limited by the algorithms listed below. Generate a list of SPRS's for
all known primes and do pattern matching/search algorithms to look for
trends that will limit the search scope. The algorithms might even
include SPRS orderings recursively. ------------------------------
Here are the rules that govern abcd: If nmp > aptnmp, then a = left. If
nmp < aptnmp, then a = right. If nmp = aptnmp, then a = same. If N - 1's
"a" = left, and N's "a" = right, then set N's "a" = LR. If N - 1's "a" =
right, and N's "a" = left, then set N's a = RL. If N's nmp - (N - 1)'s
nmp > 0, then b = pos. If N's nmp - (N - 1)'s nmp < 0, then b = neg. If
C = same, then b = null. Meaning, if N's nmp - (N-1)'s nmp = 0, then b=
null. If N's nmp - (N-1)'s nmp is an even integer, then c = even. If N's
nmp - (N - 1)'s nmp is an odd integer, then c = odd. If N's diff > (N -
1)'s diff, then d = up. If N's diff < (N - 1)'s diff, then d = down. If
N's diff = (N-1)'s diff, then d = same. If (N - 1)'s diff > 1 and N's
diff = 1, then d = reset. If (N - 1)'s diff = 1 and N's diff > 1, then d
= undoreset. [......But maybe when (N - 1)'s diff and N's diff = either
1 or 3, then d would also = up, or d = down.] If a = left or RL, then N
prime = nmp:aptnmp, diff = |nmp - aptnmp| If a = right or LR, then N
prime = aptnmp:nmp, diff = |nmp - aptnmp| If a = same, then N prime =
nmp:nmp, diff = |nmp - aptnmp|, but only when N prime = N.
------------------------------ Copyright 10/24/2004 Justin Coslor
Prime number patterns based on a ratio balance of the largest
near-midpoint prime number and the non-prime combinations of factors in
the remainder: An overlay of symmetries describe prime number patterns
based on a ratio balance of the largest near midpoint prime number and
the non-prime combinations of factors in the remainder. This is to cut
down the search space for the next prime number, by guessing at what
range to search the prime in first, using this data.

For instance, we might describe the prime number 67 geometrically by
layering the prime number 31 under the remainder 36, which has the
modulo binary symmetry equivalency of the pattern 2*2*3*3. We always put
the largest number on top in our description, regardless of whether it
is prime or non-prime, because this ordering will be of importance in
our sentence description of that prime.
   We describe the sentence in relation to how we described the prime
number that came before it. For instance, we described 61 as 61=31:2*3*5
ratio (the larger composite always goes on the left of the ratio symbol,
because it will be important to note which side the prime number ends up
on), difference of 1 (difference shows how far from the center the
near-mid prime lies. 31-30=1), right->left (this changing of sides is
important to note because it describes which side of the midpoint of the
prime that the nearest-to-midpoint prime lies on or has moved to, in
terms of the ratio symbol) odd same (this describes whether the
nearest-to-midpoint primes of two prime numbers have a difference that
is even, odd, or if they have the same nearest-to-midpoint primes.)
67=2*2*3*3:31 ratio, difference of 5, left->right same undo last reset.
By looking at the pattern in the sentence descriptions (180 possible
sentences), we can tell which side of the ratio sign that the next
prime's nearest-to-midpoint prime lies on, which tells you which half of
the search scope the next prime lies in, which might cut the
computational task in finding the next finding that next prime number in
half or more. A computer program to generate these sentences can be
written for doing the pattern matching. In the prime number 67 example,
the part that says "same", refers to whether the nearest-to- midpoint
primes of two prime numbers have a difference that is even, odd, or if
they have the same nearest-to-midpoint primes. I threw in the "reset to
1" thing just because it probably occurs a lot, then there's also the
infamous "undo-from-last-reset" which it brings the difference from 1
back to where it was previously at. Copyright 10/5/2004 Justin Coslor
Prime Numbers in Geometry continued . . . Modulo Binary I think that if
prime numbers can be expressed geometrically as ratios there might be a
geometric shortcut to determining if a number is prime or maybe
non-prime. Prime numbers can be represented symmetrically, but not with
colored partitions. (*See diagrams.) Here's a new kind of binary code
that I invented, based on the method of partitioning a circle and
alternately coloring and grouping the equiangled symmetrical partitions
of non-prime partition sections. (*Note, since prime numbers don't have
symmetrical equiangled partitions, use the center-number + offset
converted into modulo binary (see my 2/4/2005 idea and the 2/1/2005
diagram I drew for prime odd and even cardinality and data compression
on the prime numbers)). Modulo binary: *Based on geometric symmetry
ratios. **I may not have been very consistent with my numbering scheme
here, but you should be in final draft version. 1=1 2=11 3=111 4=1010
5=11111 6=110110 or 101010 7=1111111 8=10101010 9=110110110
10=1010101010 11=11111111111 12=110110110110 13=1111111111111
14=10101010101010 15=10110,10110,10110 16=1010,1010,1010,1010 Find a
better way of doing this that might incorporate my prime center number +
offset representation of the primes and non-primes. This is an entirely
new way of counting, so try to make it scalable, and calculatable.
Secondary Levels of Modulo Binary: (*This is just experimental. . .I
based these secondary levels on the first level numbers that are
multiples of these.) 0=00 1=1 2=10 3=110 4=2+2=1010 5=10110 6=3+3=110110
or 111000 or 101101 7= 8=4+4=10101010 9=3+3+3=110110110 10=1010101010
11= 12=3+3+3+3=110110110110 13= 14=10101010101010101010
15=5+5+5=101101011010110 16=4+4+4+4=1010101010101010 Draw a 49 section

and 56 section circle, and look for symmetries to figure out how best to represent the number 7 in the secondary layer of modulo binary. There needs to be a stop bit too. Maybe 00 or something, and always start numbers with a 1. The numbers on through ten should be sufficient for converting partially from base 10. Where calculations would still be done in base 10, but using modulo binary representations of each digit. For encryption obfuscation and stuff. It seems that for even numbers, the half-circle symmetries rotate between 0,0 across the circle for numbers that are odd when divided by two, and the numbers that are odd when divided by two have alternate-half 0,0 symmetry. But numbers that are prime when divided by two have middle- across 0,1 symmetry. Copyright 9/30/2004 Justin Coslor Prime Numbers in Geometry *Turn this idea into a Design Science paper entitled "Patterns in prime composite partition coloring structures". In the paper, relate these discoveries to the periodic table. (All prime numbers can be represented as unique symmetries in Geometry.) 1/1 = 0 division lines 1/2 = 1 division lines 1/3 = 3 division lines 1/4 = 2 division lines 1/5 = 5 division lines 1/6 = 5 division lines = one 1/2 division line and two 1/3 division lines on each half circle. 1/7 = 7 division lines 1/8 = 4 division lines 1/9 = _____ division lines . . . Or maybe count by partition sections rather than division lines. . . How do I write an algorithm or computer program that counts how many division lines there are in a symmetrically equiangled partitioning of a circle, where if two division lines that meet in the middle (as all division lines do) form a straight line they would only count as one line and not two? Generate a sequential list of values to find their number of division lines, and see if there is any pattern in the non-prime division line numbers (i.e. 1/4, 1/6, 1/8, 1/9, 1/10, 1/12, ...) that might be able to be related to the process of determining or discovering which divisions are prime, or the sequence of the prime numbers (1/2, 1/3, 1/5, 1/7, 1/11, 1/13, 1/17, ...). 10/5/2004 Justin Coslor As it turns out, there is a pattern in the non-prime division lines that partition a circle. The equiangled symmetry partition patterns look like stacks of prime composites layered on top of one another like the Tower of Hanoi computer game, where each layer's non-prime symmetry pattern can be colored using it's own colors in an on-off configuration around the circle (See diagrams.). Prime layers can't be colored in an on-off pattern symmetrically if the partitions remain equiangled, because there would be two adjacent partitions somewhere in the circle of the same color, and that's not symmetrical. Copyright 7/25/2005 Justin Coslor Geometry of the Numberline: Pictograms and Polygons. (See diagrams)

Obtain a list of sequential prime numbers. Then draw a pictogram chart for each number on graph paper, with the base 10 digits 1 through 10 on the Y-axis, and on the X-axis of each pictogram the first column is the 1's column, the second column is the 10's column, the third columns is the 100's column, etc. Then plot the points for each digit of the prime number you're representing, and connect the lines sequentially. That pictogram is then the exact unique base-10 geometrical representation of that particular prime number (and it can be done for non-prime numbers too). Another way to make the pictogram for a number is to plot the points as described, but then connect the points to form a maximum surface area polygon, because when you do that, that unique polygon exactly describes that particular number when it's listed in its original orientation. inside the base-10 graph paper border that uses the minimum amount of X-axis boxes necessary to convey the picture, and pictograms are always bordered on the canvas 10 boxes high in base 10. Other bases can be used too for different sets of pictograms. What does the pictogram for a given number look like in other bases? We can connect the dots to make a polygon too, that is exactly the specific representation in its proper orientation of that particular unique number represented in that base. Also I wonder what the pictograms and polygon pictograms look like when represented in polar coordinates?

These pictogram patterns might show up a lot in nature and artwork, and it'd be interesting to do a mathematical study of photos and artwork, where each polygon that matches gets bordered by the border of it's particular matching pictogram polygon in whatever base it happens to be in, and pictures might be representable as layers of these numerical pictograms, spread out all over the canvas overlapping and all, and maybe partially hidden for some. You could in that way make a coordinate system in which to calculate the positions and layerings of the numerical pictograms that show up within the border of the photo or frame of the artwork, and it could even be a form of steganometry when intentionally layered into photos and artwork, for cryptography and art.

Summing multiple vertexes of numerical polygon pictograms could also be used as a technique that would be useful for surjectively distorting sums of large numbers. That too might have applications in cryptography and computer vector artwork.

See the diagram of the base 10 polar coordinate pictogram representation of the number 13,063. With polar notation, as with Cartesian Coordinate System notation of the pictograms, it's important to note where the reference point is, and what base it's in, and whether it's on a polar coordinate system or Cartesian Coordinate System. In polar coordinates, you need to know where the center point is in relation to the polygon. . .no I'm wrong, it can be calculated s long as no vertexes lie in a line. In all polygon representations, the edge needs to touch all vertexes. Copyright 7/27/2005 Justin Coslor Combining level.group.offset hierarchical representation with base N pictogram representation of numbers (See diagrams)

level.group offset notation is (baseN^level)*group+offset Pictogram notation is as described previously.

If you take the pictogram shape out of context and orient it differently it could mean a lot of different things, but if you know the orientation (you can calculate the spacing of the vertexes in different orientations to find the correct orientation, but you know must also know what base the number is in to begin with) then you can decipher what number the polygon represents. You must know what the base is because it could be of an enormous base. . .you must also know an anchor point for lining it up with the XY border of the number line context in that base because it could be a number shape floating inside a enormous base for all anyone knows, with that anchor point. Also, multiple numbers on the same straight line can be confusing unless they are clearly marked as vertexes. If multiple polygons are intersecting, then they could represent a matrix equation of all of those numbers. Or if there are three or four polygons connected to each other by a line or a single vertex, then the three pictograms might represent the three or four parts of a large or small level.group.offset number in a particular base. Pictograms connected in level.group offset notation would still need to be independently rotated into their correct orientation, and you'd need to know their anchor points and base, but you could very simply represent an unfathomably enormous number that way in just a tiny little drawing. Also, numbers might represent words in a dictionary or letters of an alphabet. This is literally the most concise way to represent unfathomably enormous numbers that possibly anyone has ever imagined. Ever. You could write a computer program that would draw and randomize these drawings as a translation from a dictionary/language set and word processor document. They could decoded in the reverse process by people who know the anchor point keys and base keys for each polygon. You can make the drawings as a subtle off-white color blended into the white part of the background of a picture, and transmit enormous documents as a single tiny little picture that just needs some calculating and keys to decode. Different polygon pictograms, which each could represent a string of numbers, which can be partitioned into sections that each represents a word or character, could each be drawn in a different color. So polygons that are in different colors and different layers in a haphazard stack, could be organized, where the color of multiple polygons, means they are part of the same document string, and the layering of the polygons indicates the order that the documents are to be read in. Copyright 7/28/2005 Justin Coslor Optimal Data Compression: Geometric Numberline Pictograms

If each polygon is represented using a different color, you don't even need to draw the lines that connect the vertexes, so that you can cram as many polygons as possible onto the canvas. In each polygon, the number of vertexes is the number of digits in whatever base it's being represented in. Large bases will mean larger image dimensions, but will allow for really small representations of large numbers. Ideally one should only use a particular color on one polygon once. For optimal representation, one should represent each number in a base that is as close to the number of digits in that base as possible. If you always do that, then you won't have to know what base the polygon is represented in to begin with (because it can be calculated). However, you will still need to know the starting vertex or another anchor point to figure out which orientation the polygon is to be perceived of in. On polar coordinate polygon pictograms, you will just need to know the center point and a reference point such as where the zero mark is, as well as what base the polygon is represented in (in most cases). Hierarchical level.group.offset data compression techniques or other data compression techniques can also be used. Copyright 7/24/2005 Justin Coslor Prime Inversion Charts (See diagram) Make a conversion list of the sequential prime numbers, where each number (prime 1 through the N'th prime) is inverted so that the least significant digit is now the most significant digit, and the most significant digit is now the least significant digit (ones column stays in the ones column, but the 10's column gets put in the 10ths column on the other side of the decimal point, same with hundreds, etc.). So you have a graph that goes from 0 through 10 on the Y-axis, and 0 through N along the X axis, and you just plot the points for prime 1 through the N'th prime and connect the dots sequentially. Also, you can convert this into a binary string by making it so that if any prime is higher up on the Y-axis than the prime before it, it becomes a 1, and if it is less than the prime before it, it becomes a 0. Then you can look for patterns in that. I noticed many recurring binary string patterns in that sequence, as well as many pallendrome string patterns in that representation (and I only looked at the first couple of numbers, so there might be something to it). 10/8/2004 Justin Coslor Classical Algebra (textbook notes) Pg. 157 of Classical Algebra fourth edition says: The Prime Number Theorem: In the interval of 1 through X, there are about $X/LOGeX$ primes in this interval. $P=X/LOGeX$ scope: $(1,X)$ or something. The book claims that they cannot factor 200 digit primes yet. In 1999 Nayan Hajratwala found a record new prime $2^{6972593} - 1$ with his PC. It's a Mersenne Prime over 2 million digits long. This book deals a lot with encryption. I believe that nothing is 100% secure

except for the potential for a delay. On pg. 39 it says "There is no
known efficient procedure for finding prime numbers." On pg. 157 it
directly contradicts that statement by saying: "There are efficient
methods for finding very large prime numbers." The process I described
in my 10/7/2004 journal entryis like the sieve of Eratosthenes, except
my method goes a step farther in making a continuously augmented filter
list of divisor multiplicants not to bother checking, while
simultaneously running the Sieve of Eratosthenes in a massive
synchronously parallel computational process. Prime numbers are useful
for use in pattern search algorithms that operate in abdicative and
deductive reasoning engines (systems), which can be used to explore and
grow and help solve problems and provide new opportunities and to invent
things and do science simulations far beyond human capability. (Pg. 40)
Theorem: An integer $x>1$ is either prime or contains a prime factor
$<=sqrt(x)$. Proof: $x=ab$ where a and b are positive integers between 1 and
x. Since P is the smallest prime factor, $a>=p$, $b>=p$ and $x=ab>=p^2$. Hence
$p<=sqrt(x)$. Example: If $x=10$ $a=2$ and $b=5$. $p=3$ $p^2=9$ so $10=2*5>=9$. So
factors of x are within the scope of $(2, sqrt(x))$ or else it's prime.
$a^2>=b^2$. $x^2>=p^4$. $x^2/p^4=big$. Try converting Fermat's Little Theorem
and other corollaries into geometry symmetries and modulo binary format.
The propositions in Modern Algebra about modulo might only hold for two-
dimensional arithmetic, but if you add a 3rd dimension the rotations are
countable as periods on a spiral, which when viewed from a perpendicular
side-view looks like a 2-dimensional waveform. 9/26/2004 Justin Coslor
Privacy True privacy may not be possible, but the best that we can hope
for is a long enough delay in recognition of observations to have enough
time and patience to put things intot the perspective of a more
understanding context. Copyright 9/17/2004 Justin Coslor A Simple,
Concise, Encryption Syntax. This can be one layer of an encryption, that
can be the foundation of a concise syntax. *Important: The example does
not do this, but in practice, if you plan on using this kind of
encryption more than once, then be sure to generate a random unique
binary string for each letter of the alphabet, and make each X digits
long. Then generate a random binary string that is N times as long as
the length of your message to be sent, and append unique sequential
pieces (of equal length) of this random binary string to the right of
each character's binary representation. The remote parts should have
lots of securely acquired random unique alphabet/random binary string
pairs, such as on a DVD that twas delivered by hand. In long messages,
never use the same alphabet's character(s) more than once but rotate to
the next binary character representation on the DVD sequentially. Here's
the example alphabet (note that you can of course choose your own
alphabetic representation as long as it is logically consistent): a
010101 b 011001 c 011101 d 100001 e 100101 f 101001 g 110001 h 110101 i
111001 --------- j 010110 k 011010 l 011110 m 100010 n 100110 o 101010 p
110010 q 110110 r 111010 --------- s 010111 t 011011 u 011111 v 100011 w
100111 x 101011 y 110011 z 110111 space 111011 ----------------------
EXAMPLE: "peace brother" can be encoded like this using that particular
alphabet:
011011101001011000101101011100100110010110010101110111011011010010110111011010110
0101111010101010100001101110110101111001010111101001
----------------------- 2/18/2005 Update by Justin Coslor Well, I
forgot how to break my own code. Imagine that! I think it had something
to do with making up a random string that was of a length that is
divisible by the number of letters in the alphabet, yet is of equal
bit-length to the bit-translated message, so that you know how long the
message is, and you know how many bits it takes to represent each

character in the alphabet. Then systematically mix in the random bits with the bits in the encoded message. In my alphabet I used 27 characters that were each six bits in length; and in my example, my message was 13 characters long, 11 of which were unique. I seriously have no idea what I was thinking when I wrote this example, but at least my alphabet I do understand, and it's pretty concise, and sufficiently obscured for some purposes. Copyright 6/30/2005 Justin Coslor Automatic Systems (See Diagram) There is 2D, and there are 3D snapshots represented in 2D, and there is the model-theory approach of making graphs and flowcharts, but why not add dimensional metrics to graph diagrams to represent systems more accurately?
---------------------------- Atomic Elements -> Mixing pot -> Distillation/Recombination: A->B->C->D->E -> State Machine Output Display (Active Graphing = real-time) -> Output Parsing and calculation of refinements (Empirical) -> Set of contextually adaptive relations: R1->A, R2->B, R3->C, R4->D, R5->E. ------------------------------------ Copyright 5/11/2005 Justin Coslor How to combine sequences: Draw a set of Cartesian coordinate system axis, and on the x axis mark off the points for one sequence, and on the y axis mark off the points for the sequence you want to combine with it (and if you have three sequences you want to combine, mark off the third sequence on the z-axis. ...for more than 3 sequences, use linear algebra). Next draw a box between the origin and the first point on each sequence; then calculate the length of the diagonal. Then do the same for the next point in each sequence and calculate the length of the diagonal. Eventually you will have a unique sequence that is representative of all of the different sequences that you combined into one in this manner. For instance, you could generate a sequence that is the combination of the prime numbers and the Fibonacci Sequence. In fact, the prime numbers might be a combination of two or more other sequences in this manner, for all I know. 1/4/2005 Justin Coslor Notes from the book "Connections: The Geometric Bridge Between Art and Science" + some ideas.

In a meeting with Nehru in India in 1958 he said "The problem of a comprehensive design science is to isolate specific instances of the pattern of a general, cosmic energy system and turn these to human use." The topic of design science was started by architect, designer, and inventor Buckminster Fuller. The chemical physicist Arthur Loeb, who considers design science to be the grammar of space. Buy that book, as well as the book "The Undecidable" by Martin Davis.

Chemist Istvan Hergittai edited two large books on symmetry. He also edits the journals "symmetry" and "space structures" where I could submit my paper on the geometry of prime numbers and patterns in composite partition coloring structures. *Also, send it to Physical Science Review to solicit scientific applications of my discovery. Send it to some math journals too. Again, the paper I want to write is called "Patterns in prime composite partition coloring structures", and it will be based on that journal entry I had about symmetrically dividing up a circle into partitions, then labeling the alternating patterns in the symmetries using individual colors for each primary pattern in the stack, similar to that game "The Tower of Hanoi". Study the writings of Thales (Teacher of Pythagoras), who is known as the father of Greek mathematics, astronomy, and philosophy, and who visited Egypt to learn its secrets [Turnbull, 1961 "The Great Mathematicians], [Gorman, 1979 Pythagoras - A Life] ---------------------------- Connections page 11. Figure 1.7 The Ptolemaic scale based on the primes 2, 3, and 5. C=1, D=8/9, E=4/5, F=3/4, G=2/3, A=3/5, B=8/15, C=1/2.
----------------------- Figure 1.6 The Pythagorean scale derived from

the primes 2 and 3: C=1, space=8/9, D=8/9, space=8/9, E=64/81, space=243/256, F=3/4, space=8/9, G=2/3, space=8/9, A=16/27, space=8/9, B=128/243, space=243/256, C'=1/2, space=8/9, D'=4/9, space=8/9, E'=32/81, space=243/256, F'=3/8, space=8/9, G'=1/3, space=8/9, A'=8/27, space=8/9, B'=64/243, space=243/256, C"=1/4. ---------------- *1/4/2005 Project:

Someday try writing an electronic music song that makes vivid use of parallel mathematical algorithms based on the prime numbers, actually come to think of it, this concept was presented in an episode of Star Trek Voyager. -------------------------- 8/26/2004 Justin Coslor Notes (pg. 1) These are my notes on three papers contributed to the MIT Encyclopedias of Cognitive Science by Wilfried Sieg in July 1997: Report CMU-PHIL-79, Philosophy, Methodology, Logic. Pittsburgh, Pennsylvania 15213-3890. - Formal Systems - Church Turing Thesis - Godel's Theorems ----------------------------- Notes on Wilfried Sieg's "Properties of Formal Systems" paper: Euclid's Elements -> axiomatic-deductive method. Formal Systems = "Mechanical" regimentation of the inference steps along with only syntactic statements described in a precise symbolic language and a logical calculus, both of which must be recursive (by the Church-Turing Thesis). Meaning Formal Systems use just the syntax of symbolic word statements (not their meaning), recursive logical calculus, and recursive symbolic definitions of each word.

Frege in 1879: "a symbolic language (with relations and quantifiers)" + an adequate logical calculus -> the means for the completely formal representation of mathematical proofs. Fregean frame -> mathematical logic ->Whitehead & Russell's "Principia Mathematica" -> metamathematical perspective <- Hilbert's "Grundlagen der Geometrie" 1899 *metamathematical perspective -> Hilbert& Bernays "Die Prizipien der Mathematik" lectures 1917- 1918 -> first order logic = central language + made a suitable logical calculus. Questions raised: Completeness, consistency, decidability. Still active. Lots of progress has been made in these areas since then. **Hilbert & Bernays "Die Prizipien der Mathematik" lectures 1917-1918 -> mathematical logic. Kinds of completeness: Quasi-empirical completeness of Zermelo Fraenkel set theory, syntactic completeness of formal theories, and semantic completeness = all statements true in all models. - Sentential logic proved complete by Hilbert and Bernays (1918) and Post (1921). - First order logic proved complete by Godel (1930). "If every finite subset of a system has a model, so does the systems." But first order logic has some non-standard models.

Hilbert's Entsheidungsproblem proved undecidable by Church & Turing. It was the decision problem for first order logic. So the "decision problem" proved undecidable, but it lead to recursion theoretic complexity of sets, which lead to classification of 1. arithmetical, 2. hyper-arithmetical, and 3. analytical hierarchies. It later lead to computational complexity classes. So they couldn't prove what could be decided in first order logic, but they could classify the complexity of modes of computation using first order logic. ---In first order logic, one can classify the empirical and computational complexity of syntactic configurations whose formulas and proofs are effectively decidable by a Turing Machine. I'm not positive about this next part. ...but, such syntactic configurations (aka software that eventually halts) are considered to be formed systems. In other words, ,one cannot classify the empirical and computational complexity of software that never halts (or hasn't halted), using first order logic. The Entsheidungsproblem (First order logic Decision Problem) resulted in model theory, proof theory, and computability thoery. It required "effective methods" of decision making to be precisely defined. Or rather, it required effective methods of characterizing what could or couldn't be decided in first-order logic.

The proof of the completeness theorem resulted in the relativity of "being countable" which in turn resulted in the Skolem paradox. ***I believe that paradoxes only occur when the context of a logic is incomplete or when it's foundations scope is not broad enough.

Semantic arguments in geometry yielded "Relative Consistency Proofs". Hilbert used "finitist means" to establish the consistency of formal systems. Ackerman, von Neumann, and Herbrand used a very restricted induction principle to establish the consistency of number theory. Modern proof theory used "constructivist" means to prove significant parts of analysis. Insights have been gained into the "normal form" of proofs in sequent and natural deduction calculi. So they all wanted to map the spectrum of unbreakable reason. Godel firmly believed that the term "formal system' or 'formalism' should never be used for anything but software that halts.

--------------------------------- 9/1/2004 Justin Coslor Notes on Wilfried Sieg's "Church-Turing Thesis" paper:

Church re-defined the term "effective calculable function" (of positive integers) with the mathematically precise term "recursive function". Kleen used the term "recursive" in "Introduction to Metamathematics, in 1952. Turing independently suggested identifying "effectively calculable functions" as functions whose values can be computed (mechanically) using a Turing Machine.Turing & Church's theses were, in effect, equivalent, and so jointly they are referred to as the Church-Turing Thesis. Metamathematics takes formally presented theories as objects of mathematical study (Hilbert 1904), and it's been pursued since the 1920's, which led to precisely characterizing the class of effective procedures, which led to the Entsheidungsproblem, which was solved negatively relative to recursion (****but what about for non-recursive systems?). Metamathematics also led to Godel's Incompleteness Theorems (1931), which apply to all formal systems, like type theory of Principia Mathematica or Zermalo-Fraenkel Set Theory, etc. Effective Computability: So it seems like they all wanted infallable systtems (formal systems), and the were convinced that the way to get there required a precise definition of effective calculability. Church and Kleen thought it was equivalent to lambda-definability, and later prove that lambda-definability is equivalent to recursiveness (1935-1936).

Turing thought effective calculability could be defined as anything that can be calculated on a Turing Machine (1936). Godel defined the concept of a (general) recursive function using an equational calculus, but was not convinced that all effectively calculable functions would fall under it. Post (*my favorite definition...*) in 1936 made a model that is strikingly similar to Turing's, but didn't provide any analysis in support of the generality of his model. But Post did suggest verifying formal theories by investigating ever wider formulations and reducing them to his basic formulation. He considered this method of identifying/defining effectively calculable functions as a working hypothesis.

Post's method is strikingly similar to my friend Andrew J. Dougherty's thesis of artificial intelligence, which is that at a certain point, the compactness of a set of functions is maximized through optimization and at that point, the complexity of their informational content plateaus, unless you keep adding new functions. So his solution to Artificial Intelligence is to assimilate all of the

known useful functions in the world, and optimize them to the plateau
point of complexity (put the information in lowest terms), and to then
use that condensed information set/tool in exploring for new functions
to add, so that the rich depth of the problem solving and information
seeking technology can continually improve past any plateau points.

(in 1939) Hilbert and Bernays showed that deductively formalized
functions require that their proof predicates to be primitive recursive.
Such "reconable" functions are recursive and can be evaluated in a very
restricted number of theoretic formalism. Godel emphasized that
provability and definability depend on the formalism considered. Godel
also emphasized that recursiveness or computability have an absoluteness
property not shared by provability or definability, and other
metamathematical notions.

My theory is a bottom-up approach for pattern discovery and adaptive
reconceptualization between the domains of different contexts, and can
provide the theoretical framework for abdicative reaasoning, necessary
for the application of my friend Andrew J. Dougherty's thesis. Perhaps
my theories could be abdicatively formalized? My theories do not require
empiricism (deduction), to produce new elements that are
primitive-recursive to produce new elements that are primitive-recursive
(circular-reasoning-based/symbolic/repetition-based) predicates to be
used in building and calculating statements and structures, that can add
new information. To me, "meaning" implies having an "appreciation" for
the information and functions and relations, at least in part; and that
this "appreciation" is obtained through recognition of the information
(and functions' and relations') utility or relative utility via use or
simulation experience within partially- defined contexts. I say
"partially-defined" contexts because by Godel's Incompleteness Theorems,
an all-encompassing ultimate context cannot be completely defined since
the definition itself (and it's definer would have to be part of that
context, which isn't possible because it would have to be infinitely
recursive and thus never fully representable.

Turing invented a mechanical method for operating symbolically. His
invention's concepts provided the mechanical means for running
simulations. Andrew J. Dougherty and I have created the concepts for
mechanically creating new simulations to run until all possible
simulations that can be created in good intention, that are helpful and
fair for all, exceeds the number of such programs that can be possibly
used in all of existence, in all time frames forever, God willing.

Turing was a uniter not a divider and he demanded immediate
recognizability of symbolic configurations, so that basic computation
steps need not be further subdivided. *But there are limitations in
taking input at face value. Sieg in 19944, inspired by Turing's 1936
paper formulated the following boundedness conditions and locality
limitations of computors: (B.1) there is a fixed bound for the number of
symbolic configurations a computor can immediately recognize; (B.2)
there is a fixed bound for the number of a computor's internal states
that need to be taken into account; -- therefore he can carry out only
finitely many different operations. These operations are restricted by
the following locality conditions: (L.1) only elements of observed
configurations can be changed. (L.2) the computor can shift his
attention from one symbolic configuration to another only if the second
is within a bounded distance from the first. *Humans are capable of more
than just mechanical processes. ------------------------------- Notes
on Wilfried Sieg's "Godel's Theorems" paper: Kurt Godel established a
number of absolutely essential facts: - completeness of first order
logic - relative consistency of the axiom of choice - generalized

continuum hypothesis - (And relevant to the foundations of mathematics:)
*His two Incompleteness Theorems (a.k.a. Godel's Theorems.
   In the early 20th century dramatic development of logic in the
context of deep problems in the foundations in mathematics provided for
the first time the means to reflect mathematical practice in formal
theories. 1. - One question asked was: "Is there a formal theory such
that mathematical truth is co- extensive with provability in that
theory?" (Possibly... See Russell's type theory P of Principia
Mathematica and axiomatic set theory as formulated by Zermelo...) - From
Hilbert's research around 1920 another question emerged: 2. "Is the
consistency of mathematics in its formalized presentation provable by
restricted mathematical, so-called finitist means? *To summarize
informally: 1. Is truth co-extensive with provability? 2. Is consistency
provable by finitist means? Godel proved the second question to be
negative for the case of formalizably finitist means. Godel's
Incompleteness theorems: - If P is consistent (thus recursive), then
there is a sentence sigma in the language of P, such that neither sigma
nor its negation not-sigma is provable in P. Sigma is thus independent
of P. (Is sigma the dohnut hole of reason that fits into the center of
the circular reasoning (into the center of, but independent from the
recursion)?) - If P is consistent, then cons, the statement in the
language of P that expresses the consistency of P, is not provable in P.
Actually Godel's second theorem claims the unprovability of that second
(meta) mathematical meaningful statement noted on pg. 7. Godel's first
incompleteness theorem's purpose is to actually demonstrate that some
syntactically true statements can be semantically false. He possibly did
this to show that formal theories are not adequate by themselves to
fully describe true knowledge, at least with knowledge that is
represented by numbers, that is. It illustrates how it is possible to
lie with numbers. In other words, syntax and semantics are mutually
exclusive, and Godel's second Incompleteness Theorem demonstrates that.
In other words the symbolically representative nature of language makes
it possible to lie and misinterpret.
   Godel liked to explain how every consistently formal system that
contains a certain amount of number theory can be rigorously proven to
contain undecidably arithmetic propositions, including proving that
the consistency of systems within such a system is non-demonstratable;
and that this can all be proven using a Turing Machine.
   Godel thought "the human mind (even within the realm of pure
mathematics) infinitely surpasses the power of any finite machine."
**But what about massively parallel Quantum supercomputers? Keep in mind
the boundary and limitation conditions that Sieg noted in his
Church-Turing Thesis paper of dimensional minds in relatable
timelines... (Computors). 8/26/2004 Justin Coslor Concepts that I'll
need to study to better understand logic and computation: Readings:
Euclid's Elements Principia Mathematica Completeness: quasi-empirical
completeness, syntactic completeness, semantic completeness consistency
decidability recursion theoretic complexity of sets classification
hierarchies computational complexity classes modes of computation model
theory proof theory computability theory relative consistency proofs
consistency of formal systems consistency of number theory modern proof
theory constructivist proofs semantic arguments in geometry analysis
sequent and natural deduction calculi recursive functions
Metamathematics Type Theory Zermelo-Fraenkel Set Theory effective
computability Lambda-definability investigating ever-wider formulations
primitive recursive proof predicates provability and definability
meaning: [11/11/2004 Justin Coslor -- Meaning depends on goal-subjective

relative utility. In other words, Experience leading up to perspective
filters and perspective relational association buffers.] utility and
relative utility simulation deductively formalized functions boundedness
conditions locality limitations formalizably finitist means choice,
continuum, foundations syntax & semantics incompleteness undecidable
arithmetical propositions hierarchies: arithmetical, hyper-arithmetical
(is hyper-arithmetical where all of the nodes' relations are able to be
retranslated to the perspective of any particular node?), and analytical
hierarchies hierarchical complexity computational complexity Graph
Theory Knowledge Representation Epistemology Pattern Search,
Recognition, Storage, and retrieval Appreciation

Book IV:
Invention Ideas

10/28/2004 Justin Coslor
Penny Universities
    I read in an article on the Internet that coffee houses used to be
called "Penny Universities" in the mid 1600's in England, because it
cost a penny for admission and a mug of coffee. "TIPS" is an acronym
that was posted on a tin at the counter, which stood for "To Insure
Prompt Service", and people would toss in a coin as a perk. It was a
brilliant idea when the main branch of the Carnegie Library of
Pittsburgh (nested between Carnegie Mellon University and the University
of Pittsburgh) opened a coffee shop and free Internet access terminals
this year in their library (terminals have been in place for several
years). Their renovations are beautiful! Copyright 1/1/2005 Justin
Coslor Inspiring book & some art product ideas. I've been reading the
most amazing book called "Connections: The Geometric Bridge Between Art
and Science" ISBN: 0-07-034250-4, and it's inspired me to want to read
more books on the topic of Design Science. On page 264-265 of it it
talks about the duality of Platonic polyhedra: namely The Inscribed
Sphere. face<->vertex edge<->edge p<->q Face centroids of each platonic
polyhedra are also vertex points for their duals, and so they lie
equidistant from a common center. These pages in it talk also talk about
Duality, in some of it's various forms: 1. in BartÌ3k's music - 103 2. of
maps - 125-127 3. of regular tilings - 177 4. of semiregular tilings -
181-182 5. of reciprocal figure - 224-230 6. of Platonic solids -
264-268 7. interpreting duals - 266-267 8. of convex polyhedra - 291-292
9. interpreting duals - 299-301 10. of Archimedean solids - 335-337 11.
interpreting duals - 351 12. of networks - 362-368, 370-371 13.
isometric vector matrix (IVM dual) - 370-371
-------------------------------- Product Idea #1: Copyright 1/1/2005
Justin Coslor ERASABLE DOT MATRIX SKETCH PADS WITH AN ASSORTMENT OF
VANISHING POINTS, AND THEIR CROSS-PLATFORM DO-IT-YOURSELF COMPUTER
SOFTWARE EQUIVALENT, FOR 3D PERSPECTIVE DRAWING
    Here is a product idea I came up with today. *Look at figure 6.A.2
in the book "Projective Geometry" (pg. 248-253) That picture inspired
the following idea. Here's a computer product I could sell both in
computer form, and in paper form as an artists canvas tool: make a 3D
dotted line matrix that has vanishing points along multiple parallel
horizontal lines so artists can draw realistically spacial drawings. The
dots close up are the biggest, and the dots get smaller and smaller the
farther into the background you look. Then the artist can use those dots
to realistically model 3D spacial representations on the paper, and when
they have their sketch done they can just erase the dots, because the
dots can be lightly printed on the page using erasable ink or erasable

graphite. It'd cost fractions of a cent to print out each page of this kind of drawing paper, and the paper could come in a variety of perspectives of vanishing point angles. It'd be a great product to sell archive-quality drawing pads full of an assortment 3D dot matrix vanishing point angles printed on nice white drawing paper.

On the cover of each pad there should also be a website address for where to download or order art software such as a software version of these different matrix patterns that a person can print out onto a page in very very light print (so light that it won't show up on a photocopy machine duplicate). Have some screenshots and a brochure-like visual demonstration and minimum system requirements shown on an advertisement page of how to use the software, and have that advertisement page as the first page of the sketch pads that get sold in stores all over the world. On the software brochure page (note, make the advertisement double-sided and on a perforated tear-out page that is scored for easy folding into the shape of a brochure, and use the UPC symbol as a discount coupon for $5 off of the the price of the software, when ordered online or through the mail. Include a self-addressed envelope and software payment form that can be torn out on the next page. I'd likely sell lots of software that way. On the brochure, suggest that they draw their lines on the computer paper lightly dotted matrix perspectives by hand, and that they should then either scan the page back into the computer and run it through a filter to take out the dots, or photocopy the original to take out the dots, since computer printer ink isn't erasable. This way, they wouldn't need to run to the store to buy new pads of paper. I think both of these products would be a fantastic product to sell all over the world, and I could probably get a patent on the pads. I don't agree with the notion of software patents though. I'd probably write the software using the Java3D API so that it's cross-platform. ------------------------------ Product Idea #2: Copyright 1/1/2005 Justin Coslor N-DIMENSIONAL POLYHEDRAL MOTIF DESIGNING SOFTWARE FOR ARTISTS First look at some writings by the mathematician artists from the fifteenth century, such as: Alberti, Leonardo da Vinci, and Albrecht Dĭ1Ú4rer. Then write a little computer software that makes N-dimensional polyhedral motifs (fundamental patterns) and lets the user design their own and use them as wallpaper and skins for 3D objects. So people can make M.C. Escher-like artwork easily. It'll deal with symmetry design and manipulation very easily. Copyright 1/15/2005 Justin Coslor Art Software For Making Symmetrical Design Patterns & Motifs: Write a computer graphics software that allows the user to make precise symmetry design patterns and to be able to color and shade in the sections with the greatest of ease. It could also be good for making repeatable interlocking motifs. Copyright 1/1/2005 Justin Coslor Perspective Drawing Projects When I first wrote this I was reading the book "Basic Perspective" by Robert W. Gill - Library of Congress Card Number 79-64518. 1. Try drawing a top view of an object and draw a circle of frames (Boxes) around it, and in each box draw the 3D perspective side-view of the object as it would look to a person standing on a point in the center of each frame at that particular frame's perspective angle, where each frame is a 3D perspective drawing, complete with accurate shading. 2. Draw a 3D perspective drawing form the viewpoint of a cat, and include the cat's nose, whiskers and the tip of it's tail in the drawing. Include special lighting and coloring effects such as how the scene would look if it was a snapshot from the lens of a Kirlian photography camera, as cats see a different spectrum of colors than people, and possibly auras. Copyright 1-13-98 by Justin Coslor Robotics

If one robot figures something out about it's surroundings it goes
and tells the rest, that makes available more potential actions that the
rest can do and have to work with and use as a tool. When one solves a
problem it eliminates an obstacle which each robot would otherwise have
to spend its time figuring out how to do because it communicates the
solution. Example application: new, more efficient route planner.

They could even learn teamwork too. If one robot solves part of a
problem, but knows that the whole thing isn't solved and wants to
completely solve it but not waste all day working on it, it can go and
tell the other robots about the whole problem (denoting the part they've
already solved) instead of just telling them part of the solution that
they've solved. It would also tell the other robots the estimated
"worth" (personal and societal ... sort of like a priority rating) of
getting the problem completely solved. In a sense it "asks" the others
for help. If the requested action's estimated priority is higher than
the current actions priority rating, then the robots will go and help
(fulfill the request) and in a sense perform a "favor" thus the robot in
need would be making some "friends".

Fundamental motivations: #1 stimulate/reinforce self (work towards
own goals). #2 stimulate/reinforce others. The robot might
stimulate/reinforce itself in order to stimulate/reinforce others, but
not quite as much as stimulating or reinforcing itself directly, and it
works on a "friends" and "favors" system socially. Do a favor and they
are grateful and they are your friend (and doing #2 on a friend is equal
to doing #1 and it is a random choice between the two when in question
-- when asked to return a favor for a friend or do something for
yourself). Each robot knows that it can do more faster with friends
helping, so if it has something it needs help with or is bored it might
think ahead and stop what it is doing and go out and get some friends by
doing favors for some others and then later go and ask everyone for
help. It would ask even those who aren't friends because some of them
may help and after a few exchanges of favors with them, they too might
become friends.

With a small group (approximately six robots), in order to have any
of then get any of their own stuff done you must either build a "friend
removal" system, where robots are no longer considered a friend after a
certain amount of rejections <due to probability> and they return to the
neutral "stranger" state from the perspective of the rejected robots.
Later they could easily go back into friend state though, or else have a
system of higher ignorance of the friend state rather than a 50%
favoring rate, or just have it so that they would only help a friend in
an emergency or on major projects (remember, these are robots, not
people)... Although, with only six robots it may work out to have the
standard friend/favor system without these restrictions.

So in summary, these robots would be socially interacting
communicating and sharing discovered knowledge in search of attaining
their goals. They need to be able to set goals then strive toward them,
and interact; and their goals should reflect what they are programmed to
"like" and "dislike". Their own self-discovered "likes" and "dislikes"
should always be required to be checked by multiple qualified human
operators before being allowed to be implemented. In other words all
they need are three things: 1. the ability to set and strive towards
goals (immediate and long term near future), 2. have a motivation system
(know the sensory inputs and actions that it likes and dislikes), 3. and
have a justification system (possibly a self-modifying justification
system based around a few rules and restrictions like Isaac Asimov's

three laws of robotics)... A justification system is just a way of doing things based on one's own system of what is believed to be logical, which is based on experience and the motivation/goal system, and checked by external justification systems.

These three elements are the roots of intelligent behavior. Any actions of any intelligent system/life-form can be accounted for by these three things. Copyright 1-13-98 by Justin Coslor Copyright 8/27/2004 Justin Coslor Video Game Idea

Have a digital camera + software computer or video game system that digitizes the person's physical movements, and incorporates those motions into the software or game system. Such as a game that taught people martial arts or some exercise thing. Copyright 2/8/2005 Justin Coslor. All Rights Reserved. Portable Operating Systems On Cross-Platform USB 2.0 Flash-Memory Devices This is the wave of the future in portable cross-platform operating systems. It occurred to me today while I was drinking coffee and reading a graphical book on How Computer's Work.

Design a USB 2.0 flash-memory device that only communicates using standard USB 2.0 protocols, and they would have their own software on the flash-memory that would take over the video card temporarily and have their own operating system that would load up as soon as you plug in the flash-memory card, and that operating system would be able to be minimized into the corner of the screen into a little icon, and that operating system could access all of the hardware resources of the computer, as well as all of it's software directories (using standard USB 2.0 protocols). In this manner an operating system such as Linux could be instantly loaded onto any USB 2.0 compatible computer, and it could perform cross-platform functions between its own operating system and the operating system on the hard drive, all via the independent controller drivers that were loaded into the re-initialized temporarily modified BIOS and boot record the instant you plugged the flash-memory device into the USB 2.0 port. *So it would make a new video card operating system as the primary root operating system.

Basically, the BIOS just gets re-initialized while the hard drive's operating system is running, but this time it sends special instructions to the video card to force it to buffer two (or more) operating systems transparently on top of each other, so that the user can switch back and forth between them while still seeing the other operating system(s) in the background, and either one can then be minimized into a window or icon in the corner of the screen and the mouse and keyboard could still control all of them (such as to maximize one of the operating system icons or windows) using the video card's new operating system that was instantly loaded off of the flash-memory card through the temporarily modification and reinitialization of the BIOS of the computer -- the moment you plugged in the USB 2.0 flash memory card. As soon as you unplug the flash-memory card, the computer's plug&play BIOS could unload the video card's operating system and the computer hard drive's original operating system would return to normal.

Also, since USB 2.0 has its own universal standards, if multiple flash memory operating systems (different kinds) were all plugged in simultaneously, the video card's operating system would just treat them all like icons on a desktop that can be maximized with a click, or minimized with a keystroke, or turned into a movable window that can be stacked on top of or under any or all of the other operating systems that aren't minimized. Also, another keystroke would switch between operating systems as though they were windows and which ever operating system is on top is the primary active one so that they get layered like a stack. The video card's operating system can have "save screenshot to"/"print screenshot"/"copy"/"paste"/"save to" features that can be cross-platform tools that become available when you move the mouse over an object or highlight some text, or make a selection box with the mouse -- then hold down the control <CTRL> key as you click the mouse button. This sort of simple set of cross-platform functionality shouldn't need to take up more than one mouse click's menu's worth of selection choices.

This might need to be implemented in the USB 3.0 specification, whenever that comes out, if it can't currently be done using the USB 2.0 specification. Copyright 2/8/2005 Justin Coslor. All Rights Reserved. Copyright 7/17/2005 Justin Coslor Nanotechnology (see picture)

Have a nanotechnology cell composed of seven cubes linked together by hinges in a dense unit. Electromagnets on each cube can pull each hinge closed or push it open, and electromagnets on the ends and sides of each block can connect multiple structures like this together, and can connect loose dead blocks from an interconnected storage clump to the central power supply because terminals are on the ends of each face that is diagonally across from the sub-block's hinge. There is a micro-controller in the center block of each cell for intelligence, control and orientation calculation, and communications network relaying, and there is a port that links to this this micro-controller on each outward facing face. These cellular structures would be very small and could link together to form robotic systems that are reconfigurable and adaptable. A similar robotic system exists, but like my design *much* better. The hinges could elastically be fixed at various angles between fully open and fully closed by repelling the block from both sides, at an adjustable ratio of power being fed to the opposing electromagnets. In that way the blocks could also act as touch sensors, and flex sensors, and springs and solenoids, and precisely adjustable angled hinges.

There could be lots of different shapes of cellular parts for making things, like planks, rods, hinges, plates, bearings, angle units, etc. with electromagnets and/or electromagnetic hinges on the ends and/or face plates.

A vision system would be on the external control module, and could be linked to the cellular network directly or by remote control. Everything about the block structure would be automatically calculated and added to the internal representation of the unit's state model, which can be communicated from block to block on the network of linked structures sos that blocks linked in a storage clump can be reoriented and moved about, and whole multicellular structures can be relocated as a group. The cells would talk to each other so that they know where they are in the orientation system, and the controller would have the big picture so that it could tell the cells what to do on the fly. Each group of cells could then pool its computing power to run subroutine programs as multicellular unit. Copyright 7/12/2005 Justin Coslor Product idea: seed kits for suburban gardens

One way to make a product is to package several things together in the form of a kit. One such kit that would sell well in stores and be easy to make would be seed kits for people to plant a vegetable garden or flower garden in their yard. It could contain a wide variety of seeds organized inside a divider box with a little container full of seeds in each section of the divider box, where each row is a growing season (plants that grow best in a certain season will be grouped together by row); and each container will be labeled with the name, expiration date, growing season, and ideal soil pH. The kit will come with a soil tester and will recommend certain plant fertilizers, such as Miracle Grow to change the pH.

There will be a color instruction manual with photos of each plant and seed, and it'll have some drawing space where they can design the layout of their garden, and an example will be given. The manual will have gardening tips for growing each plant. Also there should be a coupon for a discount off of a Garden Claw hand-powered rototiller tool. There should also be a website address where people can communicate in topical forums and post pictures of their flowers and vegetables from the kit for other people to see. The website should also have a comment/suggestion form to help improve the product. These would be sold in major chain stores, small shops, plant stores, hardware stores, and maybe even grocery stores all across America, and maybe even abroad. There could be several varieties of kits, and the seeds would last for several years, and seeds from the plants that were planted can then be put into those same containers to stay organized for the next year. We'd specialize in perennials especially, and would only use seeds that can generate offspring of their own, to help combat evil genetic engineering companies like Monsanto, who produces seeds that grow into sterile or seedless plants. Copyright 7/12/2005 Justin Coslor Bottled Water With the latest craze of bottled water companies, I could start my own entrepreneurial venture: River Water - "From the Ghangi to the Nile!" Ocean Water - "A mix of the seven seas.", "Aaargh!" Nuclear Power Plant Cooling Tower Water - "It's energizing!" Run Off - "Mexico City's finest.", "Free heavy metal test strip included." Sleuce Juice - "Just like Star Trek -- it's recycled!" Red Tide - "Be a man!", "Nature in a can!" Dead Sea Colloidal Brew - "Free Bible included!" Copyright 6/29/2005 Justin Coslor Camping Stuff You can make a make-shift backpack made out of a sheet: 1. Start out with a sheet. 2. Fold the sheet in half to make the pocket. 3. Tie the two adjacent corners on each side of the sheet into a knot to make the arm-hole shoulder straps. 4. There's a big pocket in the back with an opening on the top. It's a one-pocket backpack. (See Diagram) ------------------------------- A simple four stick shelter can be made from a tarp or parachute, some rope, and some sticks that are lodges securely in the ground. Tie rope around in a square with an "X" in it on the tops of the sticks, this will help support the tarp. The corners of the tarp should be tied to the bottom of each of the four sticks so that it doesn't blow away. The top of the shelter can be used to collect rainwater or dew. If you have a clear tarp this makes a great big solar still. A black tarp under a white tarp will keep you cool. To enter or exit the shelter just lift up and edge and crawl in or untie one corner and go in that way. Prop a stick under one edge to make a breathing hole. (See Diagram) Copyright 6/29/2005 Justin Coslor Cooling Shirt

The simplest way to make a cooling shirt would be to have a stretchy tee-shirt crossed with a fishing vest (for the extra pockets), and have water pockets all over it, connected by a tube (or not, in case one leaks), and make the pockets out of a kind of plastic that breathes moisture through the plastic's pores, so that the evaporation keeps the water cold, and since the pockets are up against your skin, you stay cool as a result. It'd be very simple that way and wouldn't require electricity, and there could be a rubber tube at the bottom with a valve on it so that you can drink the water right out of the cooling shirt you're wearing. This would GREAT for use in hot climates, especially in combination with water purification tablets, and there needs to be a simple system for cleaning the vest such as filling it with hot salt water and letting it sit for a few minutes. Copyright 6/27/2005 Justin

Coslor Dune Shirt (See Diagram)
    Engineer a still suit/dune shirt for staying cool. It would look
like a cross between a fishing vest and a tee-shirt, with some
attachments. It would have a water reservoir, a pump, tubes, bladders,
and a rechargeable battery pack to run the pump. The battery pack could
be recharged by a solar- power photovoltaic umbrella that could be held
by the wearer to provide shade (it might even have a little fan inside
it). The solar-power photovoltaic umbrella could also be made so that it
could be clipped onto a backpack so that the wearer has both hands free.
    If the pump is to be mechanically powered, it might be powered by
ratcheting a spring and small vertical flywheel by swinging your arms
back and forth. In that case, there might be a sort of exoskelleton that
clips a a thing onto each arm just above each elbow, and connecting it
to an exo-ribcage structure for support and making the mechanical energy
transfer. Copyright 6/29/2005 Justin Coslor Alternative Energy System
for homes that have an acre or more.
    Have habitat and employment and food/water/coffee procurement for
modern migrators. That's a different topic though...
    Live near the coast because it doesn't freeze there, and you can eat
fish and seafood. Build a yurt by the ocean and use wind power or tidal
power to purify water and provide electricity. Hip waders, sweatpants,
wool socks, and a fishing pole are essential, + a waterproof raincoat
and a sweater. Have a large greenhouse garden and do hydroponics.
    Just have a farm with a fantastic garden, orchard, and berry bushes.
Map out what grows in what seasons and in what soil conditions, and
terraform the land into the ideal form. Maybe even use terraces and
build a huge solar oven and use photovoltaics and wind turbines, but
instead of using batteries to store the energy generated (since
batteries are toxic), use water as an energy storage mechanism, either
in the form of doing electrolysis and compressing the gases into tanks
(which is dangerous) for future use in fuel cells, or the safer method
of pumping the water far uphill into a reservoir or water tower out of a
well or other water source, then have a hydropower turbine to convert
the down-flowing water into electrical power or mechanical energy as
needed, and it could drain right back into a well or onto crops.
    For a combined alternative energy system,build a huge high water
tower and put oil drum s- rotor wind turbines all up and down it and
around it, with a car alternator connected to each one, and put
photovoltaics on the roof of it and have it situated right over top of a
well or stream. Electric energy generated by from the wind turbines and
photovoltaics would be stored by pumping water out of the well into the
water tower and it can be used for plumbing from there, or it can be
used converted back into electricity by letting the water flow out of
the tower through a hydropower turbine and back into the well, or onto
the garden. You might actually get more energy out of this than you put
into it because of the hydropower dam effect that pushes the water out
with great force due to the height of the water inside the tank. Look up
plans for how to build Savonius oil drum S-rotor wind turbines. (See
diagram) Copyright 6/18/2005 Justin Coslor Pictograph books for language
adaptation.
    There should be a set of pictographs to use for icons for the main
functions of life in general. That way translations would be fairly
simple in whatever languages are used thousands of years from now. It
would be sort of like a visual dictionary. Actually, a new art form
could be created which is made of cartooning strips and comic books
without words, and you could see how complex and simple the concepts can
get beyond what words can express, though not always apparent to the

casual observer. I don't intend for such an art to replace written language, but merely for each artwork/book to be used as a teaching tool for teaching people different languages, and for inventing new languages. There would be a set of most popular (classic) books which when combined would cover much or most of the cases of describable language and basic experience that all people (including aliens) could reference to indicate a word or concept. Copyright 6/18/2005 Justin Coslor Knowledge lifespans and pictograph software

We need more mechanisms to improve the quality, quantity, clarity, simplicity, beauty, accessibility, and efficiency of knowledge that we have available to us. Hopefully by doing so we will improve the lifespan of the knowledge so that it may be found useful for many more generations than it is in its current form. There may be other steps that can be taken to improve the lifespan of public knowledge, and steps to ensure that private knowledge is in line with public knowledge, and not in contradiction..

Pictograph software:

This relates to my pictograph book idea. Maybe a computer software could be made that accepts stories and documents and written language in any written language as input, and could output a vivid pictographic comic strip or pictographic video onto the monitor or out the printer. It could also have pointer arrows to the different aspects of the pictographs which when clicked, says the literal translation into another language. Or, in the pictographic movie sequence, the audio track could be in the new language at an easy understandable pace, along with pointer arrows. Checkout Simple English: simple.wikipedia.org. An example could be done from Simple English to pictographs to another language. Copyright 6/16/2005 Justin Coslor Industries, Priority Systems, and Adaptation

Industries, much like the mind (or all life for that matter), operate under the guidance of constantly-updating priority systems. However the difference is that a given industry may be governed by the union of a wide variety of priority systems, when a singular mind may strive to adapt its priority system into every situation it encounters.

Different systems often have at least some different axioms, and in attempts to merge them, sometimes axioms need to be dropped or adopted. By merging systems, they then become more complex to adapt, but are more versatile as a result.

There is much more to an industry than supply and demand, because many variables go into and relate to supply, and many others go into and relate to demand. Quality, quantity available, target audience/market and their wants and needs, manufacturing and distribution, beneficial/enjoyability rating, priority of selling and of buying the product or service, how the product or service affects other products or services, time-frame of use and possible likely re-use count, etc. Basically the factors involved are the factors of merging a new system with an existing system, and incorporating it into the priority system.

Gaining a needed capability is generally a high priority, however taking the time and effort to analyze and learn/map out what capabilities are needed or that would drastically improve things is generally a low priority. Learning how to actually obtain those capabilities is an even lower priority in many cases. However, pre-existing maps and a personal demonstration of the value of new capabilities I've heard gets about a 15% to 30% success rate if done well (since people are resistant to change). Adaptation takes time, though if you have all of the elements in the configuration you want or need right from the start, its easier to learn that system than to learn a lesser system and then make a paradigm shift into an adaptation of that system, because the two can get confused and it takes more time. It's important to keep things simple enough to prevent discouragement in any system, unless your goal is to repel people. Copyright 6/14/2005 Justin Coslor Industry Creation

In creating a new industry one must redesign a concept or broaden a context to allow for the existence and development of a new concept to re-route a network of infrastructure. Some objects are anchored, others are flexible, and others can be augmented to, or can come in quite a variety.

A sub-industry can be created by making an anchored object flexible, augmentable, or opening up a variety of alternatives. Invent a new thing for people to do that is enjoyable and/or beneficial and there lyes the potential for a new industry. So systematically map out all of the things that people CAN do, and look for patterns that can be re-applied to dependency-chart mappings of other areas. That's the analogical approach. Also if you can solve the problem of making it possible to do something that is needed or wanted, that's another route to a new industry. The other approach is the experimental scientific deductive/inductive approach of combining concepts and wiring a pattern/tool/technique/concept into the context of another field, or even to wire many things together into what will be a novel unique context that meets the simple criteria of being beneficial and/or enjoyable. The other criteria is that it should be sustainable and non-harmful to people and the environment. The possibilities for the creation of niche markets is only limited by people's initiative and creativity. Criteria for new industries: 1. Novel/unique/worthwhile 2. Beneficial/enjoyable 3. Sustainable 4. Non-harmful to people Copyright 5/27/2005 Justin Coslor Natural Gas Mining in Landfills, Using Grids of Vertical Bamboo Tubes Since someone figured out that you can collect methane gas by sticking tubes into landfills vertically, maybe they could save some money and materials by using bamboo tubes since they're very strong, and they could drill some holes into the part of the tube that goes below the surface, to collect extra gas from the sides. Then they could push the bamboo tubes down until they're less than 1 foot above the surface, and space them out about 3 feet apart in a grid, and above the surface, have re-usable plastic or rubber caps with rubber or PVC tubes connecting the bamboo tubes to horizontal pipelines, much like a computer RAM memory array structure, and there could be a safety valve on each row. Then, when the output is really low from the methane supply being depleted, they could just stack another 5-10 feet of garbage over the pipeline field after first removing the top caps & pipeline grid on the surface, and they could do it all over again with new bamboo tubes since the other ones would eventually rot and bamboo grows so easily. Maybe use timber bamboo. Also, it may be possible to grow bamboo forests over landfills, along with non- THC hemp plants as underbrush for rope and cloth, since they're both really hardy useful weeds. Copyright 5/27/2005 Justin Coslor 3-Legged Walking Robot (It Gallops) The middle leg has a knee and a duck foot for stability, and it jumps through two spider legs that each have a knee and are angled wide for stability. When the duck foot is in back it bends or ratchets the knee (which could cock a spring), and then it rapidly straightens it out to perform the jump, then cocks the knee again in mid-jump as it passes between the two spider legs, and makes a controlled fall onto the duck leg, which is now in front. The spider legs make a similar motion to get in front too, except the spider legs do the turning. To turn, one of the spider legs just bends more than the other one, or pushes harder than the other one.

It could even pull a cart. These things could be smoothly hopping along all over the place, and could be made very small or even very large. It could even climb up stairs too, and might even be able to go down stairs (carefully). Copyright 3/16/2005 Justin Coslor MAGNETOSONIC ELEMENT SEPARATOR Have six walls separate walls, each one individually attached to it's own robotic manipulator arm, so that the robotic arms can clamp the walls into the shape of a cube. Two of the walls, both opposite to each other, are to be lined with ferromagnetic electromagnets. Two of the walls, both on opposite sides, are to be lined with paramagnetic electromagnets. The remaining two walls are to be lined with diamagnetic electromagnets. Before the top wall (the lid) is put on, rocks and raw ore are to be dumped inside. In two opposite diagonal corners there are some fiberoptics units connected on long cords to digital CCD observation cameras. Each of the remaining corners is to have a sonic cannon mounted in it beamed at the wall diagonally across from it. Then all of electromagnets are to be turned on, as well as all of the sonic cannons, and so, all of the rocks and ore inside will be obliterated by the sonic cannons into powder, and then magnetically drawn to the wall that it is molecularly attracted to by the various kinds of electromagnets. Then the robotic arms will take the cube apart and dump each wall's contents into its own melting pot or storage container for further chemical separation or polymerization. This can be a very efficient way to process materials. Here I've labeled the sonic cannon-mounted corners using the letters A through F: A->side 1 = electroferromagnetic north plate B->side 2 = electroferromagnetic south plate C->side 3 = electroparamagnetic positive plate D->side 4 = electroparamagnetic negative plate E->side 5 = electrodiamagnetic negative plate F->side 6 = electrodiamagnetic positive plate. The remaining two corners are the fiberoptic view-ports. Anything that isn't magnetic at all also just gets dumped in its own vat. Copyright 1/7/2005 Justin Coslor Diamagnetic Electromagnets {Diamagnetic materials: water, salt, pyrolytic graphite, bismuth, etc.}

When you pass a magnet over a coil, or pass a coil through a magnetic field, electricity flows through the coil. Electric generators are based on that principle. Electric generators turn into electric motors when electricity is passed through them (At least the electro-magnetic rotational kind.)

So why can't we make electric generators that are based on diamagnetic materials, such as diamagnetic coils or diamagnetic electromagnets? *See the electromagnetism logic database diagram I drew that shows in the database margins what is perpendicular and parallel to what, etc, in the relations of different kinds of electromagnetic properties and devices and materials maybe. **See the different kinds of ferromagnetic and diamagnetic electromagnet designs I invented (hand-drawn diagrams 1/7/2005). Copyright 2/8/2005 Justin Coslor PDA Kiosks

Use a PDA as a remote-controlled teaching pendant for a robot, and bolt several PDA's down into a kiosk and network them for use as a head's-up display. Attach a keyboard and a switch-box to it, have a stylus on a cord, and include a printer. The great part is that PDA's turn on instantly and consume very little electricity. Networking software and hardware might need to be designed for them though, but it likely already exists.

The kiosks could be very very small this way, and could just be on a swing-arm or arm bolted to a wall or tabletop with power cord leading up to them. Copyright 8/10/2005 Justin Coslor PDA Virtual Reality/Augmented Reality System (See Diagram)

Build or adapt a lightweight sunglasses-like head mounted display
that uses high resolution LCD screens in stereo for portable virtual
reality uses with a PDA and folding PDA keyboard (it should also work on
a laptop). Even a single color high resolution LCD head mounted display
for a PDA would be incredible for reading and browsing the web
wirelessly, as well as browsing VRML and Java3D worlds at at least
800x600 color pixel resolution. Battery life is the main issue here. You
need to be able to get at least 10 hours of battery life, and it needs
to be easily rechargeable. An augmented reality transparent LCD screen
would be ideal or one of those miniature projector LCD's. Also, it might
be neat to have a wireless 3D finger ring mouse that has several buttons
on it, at least for drawing 3D models and browsing VRML and Java3D
worlds and webpages. The PDA screen could be a small scale version of
the 3D HMD scene or programmable control panel buttons. There could be a
videocamera on the HMD for doing Augmented Reality, and have a visual
dictionary pattern matching software and a 2D to 3D object
reconstruction software, as well as have a 6DOF head tracking system.
It's important that all of the hardware be open source programmable and
be openly interfacable.
     I realize the military already has contact lens versions of this
Augmented Reality display system, but this would be affordable to the
public. They also have G.W.E.N. (Ground Wave Emission Network)
Tower/Tempest brain interface systems too all over the country (for
martial law population control and clandestine "experiments", and such),
but that's another matter. Copyright 11/12/2004 Justin Coslor My eBike
Shop: Eco-Bikes (TM)(R)
     If I ever wanted to live in Pittsburgh for an extended period of
time (such as to go to Grad School later on), I could open up an
electric bicycle dealership, and fit each bike with solid rubber tires
from GreenTires.com or AirFreeTires.com, so that they wouldn't get
flats, and only sell bikes that use batteries that aren't highly toxic
(no lead-acid or NiCd batteries).It could be open in the evenings so
that I could go to class during the day, or I could hire some students
to help run it. We could do maintenance and repairs on electric bikes
too, and recycle broken batteries and recycle or re-use parts from old
eBikes sometimes.
     Most of all, they'd be affordable, and fitted with baskets and
fenders, and comfortable seats. This way, students could easily ride to
the East-End Food Co-Op & Whole Foods for groceries, carry library
books, etc, and ride all over town and re-claim the roads. It'd get the
city to put in special well-swept bike lanes all over town and to pass
enormous hit and run penalty laws for drivers to follow. We'd make a
huge push to get bike racks re-installed on all of the public transit
buses too. 1/13/2005 Justin Coslor Business ideas:
     Right now as a money maker I could retrofit people's bikes with
electric motors for a $100 fee + parts.
     I could also sell hard drives with Linux pre-installed on them for
$100 + parts (~$150). It could come with a set of GNU/Linux CD's.
     I could also sell homemade random number generators for $250. See my
journal entry dated 12/15/2003 and the drawing I made on 1/22/2005 for
details. They could be useful to staticians, scientists, and people who
use encryption technologies. The machine is capable of generating large
amounts of random seed numbers simultaneously for each cycle that it is
run. I might be able to sell it for even more. Copyright 1/21/2005
Justin Coslor Ram-Horn Handlebars for City Bikes: I think whomever
designed the handlebars on city bikes got the idea from looking at a
pair of rams horns.. As such, it would be neat to bolt a rams skull onto

the bike in place of the handlebars or make a hollow or cast mold
version to sell to ram/bicycle enthusiasts. (GNU-compatible) Copyright
1/13/2005 Justin Coslor Augmented Reality Goggles for doing X-Ray Vision
and 3D Image Reconstruction Architects could like augmented reality
goggles for doing x-ray or sonar vision and stereo 3D image
reconstruction of live video data as they walk through a building while
wearing the goggles. The goggles could be used as digitizers to map
details onto the original wireframe CAD schematics. The military already
has this, but I don't know if anyone has done an open-source
open-hardware version of this for the commercial market and archeology
gear. -------------------------------- 9/19/2004 Justin Coslor
Simple magnetism experiment: What happens when you wrap copper wire
around an insulated tube, then put an iron bar inside the tube, then run
electricity through both the copper coil, as well as the iron bar, but
from separate power supplies? What happens when you switch the polarity
of the iron bar's power supply? What electrical voltage, amperage,
resistance, and magnetism (Gaussmeter) readings do you get in each case,
and in the case where you don't energize the iron bar but only the coil?
Does the electricity running through the iron bar amplify the magnetic
field or the current of the copper coil?
-------------------------------- Copyright 9/19/2004 Justin Coslor
New Kinds of Electric Generator/Electric Motors In the diagram I drew,
you can use toroidal coils inside roller wheels that roll on the inside
of the magnet tube. Permanent magnets or horseshoe electromagnets can be
used around the outside (since they are three times stronger). The axle
is split in the middle and one end of each of the rollers' coil wire
goes to each corresponding separate half of the roller's axle, which in
turn comes in contact with the corresponding dived separate main axle
end cap, and just have a spring- loaded contact terminal on each half of
the axle. Another model could also have a split axle terminal, and could
have a frictionless magnetic bearing surface internally. 11/7/2004
Justin Coslor Batteries. In the October 2004 issue of Popular Science,
they talked about a thing where the European Space Agency and Team
Encounter allow people to pay $25 to have a photo + description get
etched onto a High Density Rosetta nickel chip and get send off into
space on a solar sail spacecraft. The chips are expected to last at
least 1000 years. Gold substrate CDROMs last about 10 years. D-Skin.com,
for $6, sells five CD skins that prevent scratches. Put a copy of my
friendly intelligence diagram on one of those nickel chips. It acts kind
of like microfiche. We might make some friends. Around 200 B.C.E.,
Parthinians in present-day Baghdad make a crude battery, an iron rod
surrounded by a copper cylinder inside a clay jar filled with vinegar.
-------> Try stacks of copper or zinc and bismuth plates separated by
two silicon rods between each junction and fill the container with
vinegar or bleach that you've added extra salt to, or use condensed
urine or something as the go-between, and put it in a tempered glass or
tempered ceramic container and attach terminals. Around 1898, size-D
zinc-carbon batteries made their debut inside a paper tube along with a
bulb and a brass reflector - which became the first "electric hand
torch". What we know of today as the flashlight.
    Would bismuth be a good substitute for carbon or graphite in a
battery? Would stainless steel be useful instead of iron in a wet cell?
Stainless steel has some toxic materials in it though. Would bismuth be
a good substitute for lead in batteries? They're similar on the periodic
table, however bismuth is nontoxic and diamagnetic. Water is a conductor
and it's in vinegar. Sodium chloride is too, and acidic fluids are often
in batteries as well. Maybe acids have extra electrons and bases have

extra holes? --------------------------------- 11/7/2004 Justin
Coslor See pg 35 of The Random House Book of 1001 Wonders of Science by
Brian and Brenda Williams. Battery idea #1:
    Do electrolysis on salt water to make bleach, which probably will
act as an acidic conductor. Then put the bleach in a glass or ceramic
jar and make a solid bismuth coil and put it in the bleach filled jar,
and take a solid zinc rod and electroplate it with magnesium or dip it
in magnesium and put it in the middle of the bismuth coil (or if a
bismuth tube is used instead, put it in the middle of that with some
space between it and the magnesium-coated zinc rod), and make some kind
of cap with a pressure release cannister and valve. It might work as a
great battery, but keep it outside just in case it leaks or explodes.
The bleach might crystallize (which is good) if you add a bunch of extra
salt to it after doing electrolysis. If it does crystallize, it's less
likely to leak. ------------------------- 11/7/2004 Justin Coslor
Battery idea #2: Drugstore battery.
    Open up a tin can and dump the contents out and fill it up with
Pepto Bismal and take a plastic cap and roll up some aluminum foil and
jam one end of it into the cap and wrap the other end of it in wax paper
and fold it over the edge. (You might have to boil the water out of the
Pepto Bismal to thicken it into bismuth.) Next wrap some more tinfoil
around the rim of the can and fold up an extension terminal from it. I
don't know if this will work at all. Copyright 10/31/2004 Justin Coslor
Diamagnetic Energy Generation Satellites
    When a coil is passed through a magnetic field it generates a
current of electricity through the coil. So, make a satellite that has a
coil made out of diamagnetic material, and at night it should generate a
current because the earth's diamagnetic field bows out on the dark side
of the Earth due to the solar wind form the sun. As the Earth turns, the
coil will be passing through that bowed out diamagnetic field. It's
necessary to use diamagnetic material for the coil because it will be
used to turn the diamagnetic field of the earth (which is between the
poles) into an electric current running through the coil. A coil made
out of non-diamagnetic material would not be receptive to the
diamagnetic field. Some examples of diamagnetic materials are pyrolytic
graphite, bismuth, water, and salt. The reason that ice floats is
because water is diamagnetic, and ice is more diamagnetic than water, so
it repels the water's diamagnetic field, and the diamagnetic field of
the Earth. One could theoretically make a gigantic coil out of ice, and
generate electricity with it.
    One could also make a satellite that could travel through the
Earth's magnetic field in its equatorial orbit, and the diamagnetic coil
would produce an electric current perpendicular to the Earth's
diamagnetic field, and it could beam the electricity back to Earth in
the form of microwaves. One could even try making a satellite that can
just sit and levitate permanently in a semi-fixed position in space on
the dark side of the Earth. The moon is probably diamagnetic since one
side is always facing the Earth. (See related pictures.) 10/7/2004
Justin Coslor Electromagnetism People say that electric fields run
perpendicular to magnetic fields, so maybe the electric force can be
thought of as the active force in atoms, while the magnetic force can be
thought of as the stabilizing force in atoms, yet the two forces
correspond to each other to balance the energy and space in an atom, as
energy is always in motion, and space provides potential for that motion
to occur, whether it be in loops, knots, spirals or
transfer/transformation to other planes, shapes, and dimensions of
energy flow pathways. I like to guess at possibilities then check

science, math, logic, and philosophy or experiment to see if I got
anything right. It's my hobby. It helps me develop intuition and
reasoning ability. 9/26/2004 Justin Coslor Magnetic Coordinates Magnetic
North is offset from True North because the Earth wobbles at an angle
that causes there to be four seasons. The Prime Meridian goes around the
globe, and on one hemisphere it travels through Magnetic North, and on
the other hemisphere it travels through Greenwich, England. It also goes
through True North and True South. Figure out where the magnetic South
Pole is. Is it split into branches? It's probably in Antarctica. At what
points on the Earth's geomagnetic field coordinates (x,y,z polar
coordinates) are there severe distortions or landmark sub-fields? Is 360
degrees optimal for calculating an oblong spheroid? The Earth is not
round, but more of an oblong spheroid. Why did the Greeks choose 360
degrees? Greek astronomer Hipparchus (~165- 127 B.C.) made a map that
included Antarctica so they must have had advanced technology then. The
map I've seen is fairly complete, but it only shows one side of the
globe. If he was able to have a complete detailed map of Antarctica way
back then, then surely he had a way to obtain a map of the American
Continents? Ptolemy's map also denoted Magnetic North & South offset
from true North & South. Where exactly is the magnetic North Pole, and
how often do the poles flip and why? Does the Moon's orbit get pushed
away from the Earth temporarily during the flipping of the Earth's
poles? Probably, since the moon is mostly made out of diamagnetic
material. That's why we always see the same face of it, and diamagnetic
materials repel both North and South Poles and like to hover over the
mid-point between them (Satellite levitation application... Read
diamagnetic levitation article in New American Scientist around this
month.) Copyright 9/23/2004 Justin Coslor Magnetic Battery Idea Steam
and gas atoms and molecules probably contain more quanta than liquid
atoms and liquid molecules, which partially utilize each other's
electron shells. Where steam and gas atoms probably have higher electron
orbits and have their own repulsive/attractive field depending on the
spin. Crystallized atom and molecule configurations probably exist
because a bunch of atoms and molecules were either compressed into a
tight area and extended the orbit of their strong force electron shells,
or possibly the atoms might have been cooled from a liquid state while
under the influence of a magnetic field. [10/28/2004 update: The
magnetic field of an atom is the stabilizing force, and the electric
field is the active force. . .probably?] Is it possible to make
crystallized oxygen or crystallized hydrogen or other gases? [Then just
add energy of the atom's particular spectroscopic frequency to liberate
the molecules out of the crystallized form. They'd probably have to be
mixed with other elements to form crystals at reasonable temperatures.]
What if they were highly ionized gases or isotopes? What happens if you
put two conductor terminals on a quartz crystal and then bolt a magnet
onto each side of the crystal independently so that the magnets repel or
attract each other? Will that provide a steady supply of electricity due
to the compression forces on the quartz crystal? It might be a way to
make a magnetic electricity battery that doesn't run out until the
magnets lose their charge. Just attach a circuit or light to something
to the terminals. 8/23/2004 Justin Coslor Toroidal EM Fields (like for
fusion. . .see attached pictures): I'm not claiming that this is
correct, but maybe some elements conduct electricity and have a magnetic
field that is perpendicular to the flow of electrons and maybe other
elements conduct magnetism and have an electric field that is
perpendicular to the lines of flux. Maybe some elements do both, and
maybe some do neither. Gravity is proportional to how active an element

is at the quantum level, coupled with how interactive it is externally. Make a toroidal field around a Peltier Stack (dissimilar metals like a battery all stacked up), and blow gases with extra electrons into the toroidal squasher and their extra electrons may travel up the Peltier stack, sort of like a battery, but it could polarize the stack and maybe could function as a power source without actually doing fusion. It could also be a kind of electron stripper. ??? Gravity is about how the energy of the internal interacts with the energy of the external. It might merely be cyclic regions of space that have greater potential for motion (for energy quanta and other cyclic space regions) than fairly neutral space regions. I believe that space holds a compression and that the function of space is potential for motion. Time is a function of motion, and matter is energy quantas swirling in compressed cyclic space regions. Maybe the space has knots in it to lock the quanta into cycles? Who knows? ------------------------------ Copyright 9/18/2004 Justin Coslor Note to self: Diodes act as one-way gates. Transistors act like adjustable-flow valves. They can be strung together to make Boolean logic circuits. ------------------------------ Copyright 9/19/2004 Justin Coslor Crystalline Memory Lattices: Maybe one could use intersecting laser beams to control the shadow-growth of semiconductor crystals for making optical circuitry or maybe some frequencies will grow lattice structures conducive to electron flow (Negative cells), while others (or pits rather than peaks) might grow structures (or carve/melt) conducive to receiving electrons (positive cells/holes). ------------------------------ Copyright 9/19/2004 Justin Coslor Super-cheap gigantic diamagnetic electromagnets: Try making an electromagnet out of ice as the conductor. Take some plastic tubing and fill it up with water, cap the ends, coil it up into a spiral, then freeze it. Then take a larger piece of tubing (wider) and freeze (or make a horse-shoe-style ice magnet). Then run electricity through the ice spiral and see if it is able to act as an electro-diamagnet (since water is somewhat diamagnetic). The lattice structure of the ice crystals might be good for holding a diamagnetic charge. Who knows??? Try it. If it works, make an enormous one. What happens when you beam light through the electrically conductive ice coil spiral? ------------------------------ Copyright 9/6/2004 Justin Coslor Supercomputer and Memory Technology Build a supercomputer out of millions of memory units of the kind I designed earlier that have no moving parts and operate optically. Locate the computer in either Antarctica or in a very cold climate, such as on a satellite that stays in the shadow of the Earth or underground on the dark side of the moon. It could be nuclear powered, or powered by a thermocouple that runs off of hot rocks (thermonuclear isotopes). use an instantaneous communication relay between it and stations on the Earth (see physics research in the book "The Dancing Woo Li Masters" by Gary Zukav). The key component to the memory units is the new kind of laser range-finder I designed when I was 16. 2/17/2005 Update by Justin Coslor: Recently I came up with the optimal geometry for an entirely new and different (and possibly better) solid-state dense nanotechnology memory geometry design. See my most recent journal entry to this date on that topic, as well as the partial diagram I drew that describes the mathematics behind it. Copyright 9/24/2004 Justin Coslor Speculation about photodiodes, photovoltaics, and the nature of energy transmission through materials.

Figure out how photodiodes work. I think they somehow convert light into electrons. That would mean that the light quanta would add energy to the diode's N-plate's electrons to bring the outermost electrons to a higher orbit around the nucleus and eventually high enough to be able to

transfer over from one atom to an orbit around an adjacent atom capable
of supporting an extra electron. When all of the atoms on the N-plate
have electrons at transferable orbits they will hop over the junction
and start filling in the orbit holes in the P-plate's atoms. When the
P-plate's atoms fill up with transferable atoms, then electricity will
flow in either direction because the N-P plates will act just like a
regular conductor. In fact, you might not even need a P-plate unless you
wanted a one-way gate effect. Probably, you would have to use a material
that has a photon emission frequency that is the same as the kind of
light that you are exposing it to, in order for the photons to get
absorbed by the electrons orbiting around that material's nucleuses. Use
electron spectroscopy to find suitable materials for the spectrums of
light you expect to use the photovoltaic cells under.
    Transparent photovoltaics could be made out of some kind of
crystallne materials (appropriately receptive to the incoming
wavelengths), and could be made very thick, where both the anode and
cathode structures could be transparent, and could be made of a
semiconducting crystalline block that has been formed while under the
polarizing magnetic field of a powerful superconductor. That way, every
molecule in the transparent crystalline block would act as a photodiode,
like miniature photovoltaic cells. Perhaps materials that do not look
transparent to us are quite transparent to their specific spectroscopic
frequencies of radiation, and that may be why they are able to "conduct"
those frequencies of radiation and in doing so, convert that energy into
electric/electron current. ???

    A New Kind of Potentiometer (which can be used as a tactile sensor)
    Details: Make it as a spring-loaded linear-action potentiometer
(variable resistor), where the farther the lever rod is pushed down,t e
more resistance there is on the current flowing across it between the
rod's conductive bearing surface, and the decreasingly (or increasingly)
conductive plate or channel that it glides on/in. It's a very simple
device, and clusters of them can be used in conjunction as sensors for
tactile kinetic force of varying magnitude, depending on the strength of
the spring at the bottom of the rod. It could be used n the finger-pads
or gripper-pads of a robotic arm. The glide plate/channel could be lined
with a carbon resistive strip similar to the one in regular slide-pots.
There could be some stranded insulated wire that comes off of the top of
the rod, and the rod itself could be insulated except for the bearing
surface. The ground wire would be at the top of the glide-plate's
resistive carbon film, so that as the rod gets pushed down against the
force of the spring at the bottom, the resistor would turn on or off
farther and farther depending on how it is designed. The conductive
bearing surface could just be a strip of metal with a rounded bend in
it, so that it has some spring action, and it could have a similar
rounded strip-spring on the back of it so that it pushes on the back
wall to exert some force in the direction of the carbon-resistive film.
Or the bearing surface could be a roller wheel with conductive
lubrication, such as graphite powder, and a back-wall spring similar to
the one just described or just have two independent bearing surfaces
opposite to each other with a hinge and a spring in the middle (although
that is an unnecessarily complex design). Or the bearing surface could
be like a miniature computer mouse ball in a cage that only travels
forwards and backwards and made out of metal. When I mentioned possibly
using a channel in some designs I meant it to be like a vertical gutter
that is rectangular, or triangular. A triangular gutter design would
probably be the easiest and most stable of the gutter designs to make,

and it would provide a lot of stability against possible twisting action of the spring-loaded vertical push rod. See the photo of the brief diagram that I scribbled for this invention. Contact me for terms of licensing, development, publication, and mass-production. JustinCoslor@gmail.com I'd like everybody to be able to buy these very inexpensively for their projects, and send samples out to university students and professors for free. All I'd like is the standard fair National average inventor's royalty percentage on the gross profit of the venture capital wholesale sales gross profit of these potentiometers and off the gross profit of the sale of improved models so that I can continue to come up with new inventions and have some spending money. I shouldn't have to be poor forever, because that causes so much unnecessary misery. It'd be wonderful if I had a better workshop and some helpers and colleages and more resources to work with. Copyright 9/12/2004 Justin Coslor

Highly sensitive tactile/optical range-finding robotic finger sensor-pads:

For rich tactile data input (robo-fingerpad pressure sensors that yield very detailed sensory input) sensors, add a stereo computer vision range-finding unit to each finger, and have slider resistor tubes that are spring-loaded under a rubbery surface skin, and make them flexible if possible. (Update Copyright 11/11/2004 Justin Coslor: Think of sea anemony-like manipulators that each have a little CCD range-finder setup and tactile sensors for precise gentle manipulations.) I could probably build a test pad out of drinking straws and little springs or rubber bands glued to pins that are soldered to either trimpots on a swivel-mount or tiny slider-resistors. The skin could be molded from liquid latex or a piece of bicycle innertube, and the stereo-cameras could be located up on the arm with fiber-optic light input extensions that go right out to the finger tip pads where they can be precisely angled to yield stereoscopic CCD range-finding data so that the fingers will each visually know how far they are from the objects they are trying to manipulate. Maybe the CCD's can be quadranted up into four distinct camera matrixes per CCD (or more), each of which would be fed light by it's own independent fiber optic cable that has an optics unit on each end....? That would bring the costs and power-consumption down dramatically because not as many actual digital cameras would need to be used to obtain the effect of having a whole bunch of independent digital cameras. Copyright 9/11/2004 Justin Coslor A cheaper kind of touch-screen for computer kiosks for 2D operating system user interface haptics and 3D augmented reality user interface haptics. Note: I suppose this is similar to the haptics in the movie "Minority Report."

Instead of using expensive breakable touch screens, why not set up a regular CRT computer monitor that has a piece of replaceable plexiglass over the monitor face, in the form of a kiosk interface whose mouse movements or click-movements are recorded by an overhead pair of digital cameras that are running an open-source stereo computer vision algorithm as drivers that utilize your own hands' movements as 3D haptics devices. If the operating system is a 2D point- and-click environment, then your index finger pointing in 3D angles will move the mouse and touching (or nearly touching) the plexiglass plate will execute a click (selection). If the operating system is a 3D environment, then perhaps all control of the environment will occur at least several inches to several feet from the plexiglass plate, and perhaps there could be an on-screen 3D animation that mirrors the hand movements, with trainable hand gestures to control different features and functions of the environment. The important thing that I must explicitly note is that the stereo cameras are to be situated on an extended arm overhead, and potentially out of reach, and that they are to be located either directly above or behind the user's head so that they are only focused on the user's hands (and not their face) because they are not to be made in such a way as to be able to digitally photograph the user's face, since that would be an invasion of privacy which could potentially be mis-used.

Also, there might be a projection onto a plexiglass plate in front of the face but behind the hands so that the hands can interact in an augmented reality environment in addition to being haptics devices for the above-described kiosk-like CRT screen's operating system. Copyright 10/29/2004 Justin Coslor Course Catalog and Skills Inventory (Software Idea)

Dig up my old note from years ago about how course catalogs can be interconnected and turned into software that inventories and sorts prerequisites and possibilities for which courses the student is qualified to take based on the courses they've taken. It would help students who aren't sure what to major in, to plan their school year, as well as help in organizing quite concretely the knowledge they've learned and the knowledge they can learn. The students can also build hypothetical models of future courses of study with the software, and can help teachers model new curriculums, and link their courses to other people's curriculums. Libraries can use it too. Also, every student should be able to see a summary page that lists one paragraph on the topics that will be, or have been covered in each course in each semester of their education, if not only just for the benefit of their memory, to see what they've learned (or haven't learned), what they're learning, and what they intend to learn (hypothetically) in the future. That way, they can easily reference their educational background later on in life, which is especially important if they are lifelong students or researchers.

Artificial intelligence reasoning engines could be made that generate comprehension tests and study guides and executive summaries for any book in any language, and they could link related materials and form historical and/or geographic timelines of the history and spread and evolution of ideas and concepts. Such software might already exist somewhere in some form.

Employers in industry might also like to look at these educational coverage charts if they're looking for knowledge of specific skills in applicants during their hiring process. Copyright 12/14/2001 Justin Coslor Portable Robotic Hole-Threading Tool for Building Robots and Stuff.

It drills a hole, then threads the hole with a tap, then runs a bolt through the hole, then puts a washer and a nut on the other end of the bolt. It might even clamp two pieces of material together while fastening them together in the above described manner. It would be a hand-held device, and someone could even make a version that's an autonomous mobile device (for use in space or factories), and another version could be a stationary tool bolted to the floor or something. There could be several different models. I originally thought of this several years ago through have not yet drawn schematics.
------------------ Components: Drill: high torque, high speed motor, use gears and speed control. Tap: stepper motor + Air nozzle to blow chips and slag away. Bolter: leveraged robo-wrist + gripper (or possibly a robotic version of one of those spring-loaded universal wrenches). Nutter: leveraged robo-wrist plus gripper. Clamp: as simple as possible, like one of those 1-turn clamps or something with rubber pads. Sensors: slag sensor detects chips and blows them away, torque sensors keep machinery from jamming and breaking. Vision keeps track of what is in

each quadrant of a laser matrix projected onto the work surface. Parts orienting system: Loads bolter and nutter and washers (part of nutter) and keeps parts oriented and organized. Copyright 11/12/2004 Justin Coslor Cottage Industry Explosion: Portable Inexpensive Manufacturing Robots for Intentional Communities In America

Make portable inexpensive manufacturing robots hooked up to an open-source computer terminal (possibly running the 3D modeling software Blender, and some business & art software) as a whole cottage industry manufacturing system that can be easily set up to refine materials and produce products that can then be sold locally and over the Internet.

People would design their own products of course, and they can be quite intricate and precise and easy to replicate due to the use of robots and computer technologies. The software would make the business part of it a snap. Design a general system and then use it to fabricate duplicates of itself, and sell and install them exclusively to people who live in Intentional Communities, so that America can win back its manufacturing Jobs from China and India, as well as keep its high-tech jobs from being outsourced. Copyright 11/5/2004 Justin Coslor Cottage Industry Stuff Print up some tee-shirts, coffee mugs, bookmarks, and refrigerator magnets of my friendly intelligence diagram. Post them for sale on the Internet. Write a little booklet that goes with the diagram, to include with each item, to help people understand the diagram. Look for a bootable linux distribution that has life-critical software and family business software. Order DSL and a bootable DVDRW drive and download a copy of Knoppix.

Build the portable computer-numeric-controlled (CNC) machining robot for carving ornamental wood furniture and paneling, and collect an archive of geometrical designs and nature patterns to use, and template concrete masonry patterns for face plates for beautifying buildings and for making sculptures and walkways. Build the originals out of clay and wood and use stereo digital cameras or a laser range-finder scanner to digitize the designs. Sell these portable CNC machines inexpensively to help Americans form cottage industries.

I could build ornate bookshelves and industrial design things that could be environmentally friendly and quite useful. I'll need a shop to use unless I just design it and have other people build it like Ikea does.

I could also sell Atmel AVR SP12 microcontroller programmer kits, and already-put-together microcontroller programmers, and I could put together an electronics assembly robot, and a very small very precise set of robotic arms for doing fine work. 11/11/2004 Justin Coslor Holographic Range-finding Orbiting Space Telescopes, for Holographic Geometric Reconstruction of Distant Celestial Objects and Celestial Systems (or point it at the Earth for Geographical Information Systems). See pg. 59 of The Random House Book of 1001 Wonders of Science, for info on how to make holographic images (depthy multi-perspective images). Do that on a much larger scale but out in space or even have the Holographic crystal on the Earth and have the space telescopes pointed either at the Earth or put distant objects in space. Use a gigantic holographic crystal that is sensitive to a wide spectrum of different wavelengths (colors). Have the holographic crystal on a slightly different orbit than the space telescopes, and the crystal should rotate slightly to capture the changing perspective of the orbiting stereo or triple space telescopes beamed at it. Put the space telescopes way out in space. This is nothing new, but the first two space telescopes could make the XY plane, and range- finding according to focal length, but add a third space telescope to do XYZ geometric reconstruction of a remote volume (the front face of the picture at least) with some distortion. The third telescope could be above and behind the other two for extra dimensionality, and that way there wouldn't be a blind spot, however in other configurations the blind spot might indicate where the readings start to become somewhat reliable. Copyright 10/29/2004 Justin Coslor Safety Skin for Robots Make a fabric-like skin of flexible tactile sensors to be put on the outside of robots, so that if a person (or another robot or obstacle) bumps into the robot or gets in the way of the robot, the robot immediately will shut down and disengage to prevent the chance of injuries to the person. This would be an additional layer of safety in addition to visual and/or sonar/IR/laser tachometer environmental sensors. Copyright 10/20/2004 Justin Coslor Free public archive of great anonymous writing and poetry There should be a website that acts as a free public archive of great anonymous writing and poetry throughout history. It could be searchable by a variety of interactive intelligent means, and offer a secure round-the-world ping-pong submission form that leaves no trail but is subject to human review as to whether it is worth archiving. Also, it should be entirely based on free open- source software that is eloquently coded and understandable and proven. Copyright 10/11/2004 Justin Coslor Precise EM field sensing nanocoil fabric Insulated conductive nanocoils could be useful for sensing electromagnetic fields very precisely. Somebody could make packets of independent nanocoils that could be laid out in a flexible fabric form (or rigid) where each coil would be processed and a numerical value would be passed to a unit of nonvolatile random access memory. Then this coil fabric, much like a curtain, could be passed through a room vertically to get a reading of the electromagnetic field strength at each point in the room. It could be useful for figuring out where to stick accupuncture needles in medical treatments too. It would also be useful for teaching people how to use their own body's bioelectric field in unison with the Earth's geomagnetic field to heal themselves and others, and to people how to harmonize such forces regardless of the situation. It seems like this kind of instrumentation and a visual augmented reality software simulation interface to this kind of sensory equipment could really improve people's awareness and mentality, and thus their lives. Eventually they could learn to sense the fields without the electronic equipment to some degree and not need the apparatus anymore to stay healthy and balanced. Already there is bioelectric feedback therapy, MEMS (micro-electro-mechanical-systems), and augmented reality technology (which is a form of virtual reality). 9/8/2004 Justin Coslor Notes on the Carnegie Library of Pittsburgh book "Agents Unleashed: A public domain look at agent technology" by Peter Wayner Copyright 1995, published by Academic Press, Inc. Agent Technology: Setting Up Secure Networks Parallel and Distributed Programs User Interfaces Being applied to agent technology: Genetic algorithms, computational learning theory, classification theory, adaptive-preference-based decision making automations, personal oracles/prodigies, power librarians (parse text, translate languages, figure out language ambiguities), emotional interface via animations, network roaming ability, and virus protection. Agents are like viruses that are designed to be helpful. Agents are often programmed in list, and controlled by TCL (Tool Command Language), and transmitted via PGP encrypted mime-encoded email. XLISP is a simple, free, microcomputer-based implementation of a subset of the Common LISP standards.

In LISP both the data and the program are stored in nested listt trees. Inside the LISP environment, agents can easily build up, execute,

and tear down data structures. In LISP there ar no pointers, memory
allocation, and deallocation is automatic, and there ar some security
holes but they're patchable to keep agents from overstepping their
bounds. Common LISP uses a hierarchy of packages, which are separate
tables of variables, functions, and their names. These package
hierarchies offer structured access to variables, and can be used to
keep incoming agents from executing any system calls or handling local
memory. LISP's debuggers can be re- tooled to send an agent back home
along with the pre and post screen of the remote LISP compiler's
evaluation loop hooks when an agent causes a memory access or system
resource error.

Some smaller versions of LISP such as XLISP-Plus have
object-oriented features called Common LISP Object System. Dynamic
linking/binding to find the latest functions is used in some versions
like Scheme, which lead to the more algebraic C-Like syntax version
called Dylan. Commercial versions of LISP compilers have extra features
and are faster than the free compilers. Even compiled LISP code is
semi-interpreted and doesn't have a direct ability to manipulate
pointers because it needs to stay mobile in memory, so compiled LISP
code is a great environment for supporting agents that can act on it.

If I plan to program Aritificial Intelligence in LISP rather than
Java, then I should buy the book "Common LISP: The Language" by buy
Steele, for hardcore LISP programming. Check out other books too and
read reviews and recommends online. There are probably some free LISP
tutorials online as well. Copyright 11/14/2002 Justin Coslor 2D
Wireframe Digitization of Digital Images for Computer Vision How would
the orientation matching algorithm work in the first three methods? (See
11/14/2002 algorithm.) Irregular objects: 2D width match 2D height match
Form a 2D square around the border of the object. Treat each pixel in
the image as an independent pivot point. For each pixel, draw straight
lines in a layer over top of the image at every possible angle that
intersect at the pivot point (all of which are as long as the longest
dimensions of the image). Measure how much of each line intersects with
the object, especially where there are two or more adjacent pixels in a
straight line. If you do this for all of the pixels you'll have a
coordinate database of angles and lengths and start and end points or
midpoints, which is very useful for forming groups by associating the
lines in the image in various ways, such as: intersection, adjacency,
parallelness, curvature template matching, and continuity of same line.
For some operations one can choose the line that intersects the longest
distance across the object. This is the longest intersecting line from
the current 2D perspective, whose midpoint is the pivot point. This is
useful for the following: at each endpoint of the longest intersecting
line draw a point. Draw a perpendicular line at each endpoint of the
line. Start out with a perpendicular line from the known schematics,
that is as long as the longest dimension of the object (at each
endpoint), and make sure that the perpendicular lines' midpoints are
centered on each endpoint. Now form a box at each half of the object and
reduce the width of the box until the outer edge touches the outside of
the object. Do this for each of the two halves of the object. Now you
have a tightly fitting box around that particular 2D object in the
image! The point of doing this is to be able to separate that object
from the rest of the image, and also to figure out the object's actual
perspective in the image, which can help at guessing 3D attributes. This
object can now be put into an object catalog, each image of which can be
rotated in 2D for matching against for doing approximative Bayesian
pattern matching that incorporates rotation attempts. (See related

diagrams from my handwritten journal.) Now rotate this box and 2D image
in the X,Y plane by N degrees about the pivot point until the box is
perfectly vertical and horizontal on the screen. Now you have the
computer show a front view of the 3D object model so that you can rotate
it forwards and backwards about the pivot point until you get the two
positions that match the length of the 2D image. Compare the two lengths
from the pivot point to the endpoints to find the longest or shortest
line for comparison to decide which of the two 3D positions to choose.
For each of these two possible positions we now want to find the two
positions in which the width matches by twisting the 3D object model,
and comparing the widest or shortest half of the box to the 3D model's
two possible width twistations to find out which width to choose. Now
you have the correct 3D perspective match of the 2D image and you know
the movements necessary to re-orient the object in reality to the 0,0,0
position. So just have the robot do it and begin again with the next
object, and the next, and the next, etc. Copyright 11/14/2002 Justin
Coslor Computer Vision Thought Build a little robot that can go around
its environment and pick things up and study them as objects. It would
need to be able to categorize, visualize, contextualize, and use
guess-work (heuristics) scientifically to discover each object's
function, unique and generalized characteristics (size, weight, shape,
color, physical flexibilities, bend points, and center of gravity),
symmetries, associated objects (around what objects is it generally
found and used with?), physics force vectors during use and storage
(this much weight pushes on the floor at these surfaces (points of
contact and interaction), material it is made out of (robot has a
portable microscope to analyze materials and to identify the presence of
cells), surface temperature (infrared vision module can help determine
what objects are alive, very hot or cold, or how much hotter or colder
they are than the ambient room temperature), internal composition (sonar
scanner with 3D computer optimization), and statistical analysis (out of
all the times it has been recognized, what is the average context of
objects & movements of it and the objects interacting with it?). For a
practical application, the robot would only need to recognize a few
objects and be able to ignore all of the rest of what it sees so that it
could focus just on what it needs to know and extract data needed to
accomplish its goal. It will need to simplify what it sees so that it
can quickly find what it is looking for. It should only store in its
memory the things that it will use frequently. It will frequently
identify a few particular objects that are in different orientations.
For this a simplified 3D wireframe model would be useful, also surface
color(s) (optional), symmetries, and center of gravity, or handles for
gripping on to (like symmetry lines). Let's say you have a mechanical
part and the vision system has a 3D wireframe model of its structure.
The robot grips its handle or its center of gravity, picks it up, then
figures out what orientation it is in. How does it figure out the
orientation? 1. It could have touch sensors like a little pin board
whose spring loaded pins reveal the shape (as a matrix of depths) while
the robot holds the part. After the shape is recorded in that
orientation, the vision system could match the shape to the 3D wireframe
model and then tell the robot arm to rotate the part in the XYZ to get
the part into 0,0,0 orientation so that it can be placed somewhere
accurately and systematically. 2. It could scan the part with a wide
laser range-finder, then match and reorient the part. 3. It could take a
digital photo (CCD camera) of the part from 0,0,0 orientation then
rotate the 3D computer model in the X,Y,Z until the part's current
orientation matches, then use an optimized X,Y,Z rotation algorithm to

find the shortest method of rotation to get from the original X,Y,Z
orientation to the desired 0,0,0 orientation, then the robot arm would
make that adjustment and place the part. 4. Use a part's tray with
little wells to catch the parts as they are shaken across the tray (like
on the SMART Cell manufacturing robotic system I use to work on at the
CMU Robotics Institute years ago). Copyright 8/7/2005 Justin Coslor
Binary Space Partition Trees
    I'm currently on page 17 of the book "Java 3D Programming" by Daniel
Selman Copyright 2002, and it mentioned using binary space partition
trees as a method of sorting relative positions of objects so that the
objects don't need to be re-sorted when the viewpoint changes. It didn't
explain how binary search partition trees work though I think it means
forming a tree of nodes for each object, where each node represents a
vertex on the object, and the vertexes are sorted by order of depth
(layering). That way multiple objects can be compared by comparing their
vertex depth, and when the perspective changes a different node on the
depth trees becomes node #1, 2, 3, etc in terms of the layering.
Copyright 8/10/2005 Justin Coslor
Data compression for 3D polygonal objects
    What needs to happen to make 3D and Virtual Reality and Augmented
Reality popular again is to have more software compatible with Google
Earth (A geo-spacial imaging software that can be used for navigation
--- which needs more functionality). But more importantly what needs to
happen is to have software that is able to represent 3D models using
hardly any data at all. Better 3D data compression is needed, possibly
like that stegonometry idea I had, where vertex coordinate systems are
represented as layered pictogram polygons (see the idea in my notes --
July 2005), where three linked polygons is a 3D point, or set of 3D
points, such as an entire 3D object's vertexes -- the first polygon
represents all of the x coordinates in a particular object. The second
polygon represents all of the Y coordinates. The third polygon
represents all of the Z coordinates successively, and form each
pictogram polygon in a different color for each of the objects in the 3D
scene. The whole thing is in the same base and on the same pictogram XY
coordinate system. The whole thing can be represented as a tiny vector
graphic such as a PNG file that represents an entire 3D rendered
mathematical model/visualization, which is very easy bitwise map which
translates directly into the 3D, so it'd be really fast for rendering
each abstract pictogram map of the object's vertex coordinates. Also, no
two pictogram polygon vertex pixels will fall on the same point in the
pictogram as long as all objects' 3D vertexes are separated by one pixel
or more in 3D space. This would be a highly compressed way to represent
the spacial coordinates of all polygonal objects in a 3D scene, in the
form of a tiny image file, and if you string together multiple pictogram
image files into a sort of a video sequence, the objects in the scene
could gradually move through 3D space sort of like a morph sequence,
into the positioning registered by the second pictogram image file in
the video sequence, etc. . .like a gif89 animation file, but as a vector
graphics image. That would save a lot of processing power and
representation space in recording and playing back 3D video sequences in
virtual reality. See my note from 6/13/2004 on information theory. In it
I translated an old paradigm of information theory into terms of
patterns in contexts. "If a set of contexts constitutes t bits of unique
information, and the set of patterns that the contexts are based on
contains less than t bits of unique information, then it is impossible
to create those contexts from that set of patterns." Well, since coming
up with this idea today about encoding 3D models, and the regular 2D

stegonometry version of it (see my other essay), I no longer believe
that this paradigm is true in all cases (such as this one, for example),
because it doesn't account for alternative perspectives of
representation of information (of patterns in contexts) which are
different and of different computational complexity, but are
analogically equivalent.

3D compression scheme

I've developed an alternative system of representing numbers (which
represents them as pictograms), which I turned into an alternative
method of representing 3D vertex coordinates of polygons. In it, each
sequential group of three digits in the pictographic polygon
representation represents the X coordinates for the vertexes from left
to right, or the Y coordinates for the vertexes from top to bottom, or
the Z coordinates for the vertexes from front to back. So in that way
depth and ordering of the vertexes is very organized and the 3D scene
can be drawn in layers very quickly from front to back so that it will
be easy to see which vertexes can be skipped due to their being hidden
around the backside of the object.

The three pictogram polygon numbers each get drawn in different
colors in the vertex map, and the three polygon numbers gets parsed into
either a set of X coordinates, a set of Y coordinates, or a set of Z
coordinates as previously described, where each partition represents the
three digit location of X, Y, or Z.

Probably what needs to happen as a next step is to make three
coordinate buffers: one for the X axis, one for the Y axis, and one for
the Z axis, and then copy the parsed sequences of groups of three
sequential digits into these buffers. Then there will either be a fourth
buffer that combines all of these numbers into a set of XYZ coordinates
representing the vertexes of the 3D object, or else the computer will
dynamically triangulate perspectives on the 3D object to be constructed,
where each sequential list of dynamically combined XYZ vertex
coordinates is generated from left to right, top to down, front to back,
based on a projection of an angular viewpoint of the original
orientation of the X, Y, and Z coordinate lists. That is how
re-orientations of perspectives get generated. If a polygonal pictogram
is to be built for each perspective, then the polygon points in the
pictogram can just be combined one column at a time for the X, Y, and Z
vertex polygons (in groups of 3 pixel column places on the pictogram's X
axis), then the vertexes just get placed on the 3D grid, and lines get
drawn between their boundary shells as a wireframe and skins get
applied.

If you wanted to get really simple you don't even have to use
pixels, you can just make an XY array of 1's and 0's, and have it 9 or
so digits high in the Y axis (2^9), and as long in the X axis as
necessary, and every group of N binary digits horizontally gets
multiplied by the level it's on in the Y axis to give you a set of
sequential X coordinates for vertexes of the object in the 3D space, and
in do the same in another XY array for mapping the 3D object's vertexes'
Y coordinates, and do the same in another XY array for mapping the 3D
objects' vertexes' Z coordinates. Then an XYZ vertex coordinate list
gets dynamically generated for each perspective of this vertex
arrangement that gets requested. That's how to make an object's vertex
map in binary rather than pixels.

Also, hierarchical representation can be applied to generating
different 3D perspective's projection calculations. By putting the
coordinates in terms of hierarchical representation (as described in

previous essays), calculations can proceed much more quickly than normal since it speeds up arithmetic by chunking the calculations into their highest powers of 2 (which the computer can calculate in one clock-cycle), times a multiplier, plus or minus an offset, which can also be chunked similarly if it is large. That would speed up 3D rendering of video sequences dramatically.

This is the format that I want to encode the vertex maps of objects in the visual dictionary I intend to build, and I intend to systematically and axiomatically categorize the visual objects in terms of qualitative and quantitative properties, and cross reference each object to a linguistic encyclopedia, thesaurus, and dictionary. Most of this work will be automated. Copyright 10/21/2002 Justin Coslor Thoughts on Computer Vision: 2D Snapshot to 3D Wireframe The Process: Open image Identify edges of objects Identify symmetries Identify duplicate objects in different configurations to fill in holes in that kind of object throughout. 3D Clues: Straight lines Corners and intersection points Arcs Complex areas: generalize areas such as wrinkles in fabric, or limbs on a plant, or grass (or just generalize by color). Random or repeating texture on flat or curved surfaces can also give clues. Guess at 2D perspective. Rotate perspective to rectalinear*. Guess at hidden areas by filling in holes. Rotate to top perspective, and guess at holes. Rotate to side 1 (*see diagrams) perspective, guess at holes. Rotate to side 2 perspective, guess at holes. Build 3D wireframe. Of any 2D picture you basically can see three sides of a cube, and may have to guess at the other three sides. It's important to note distorted areas and account for that in the image processing and representation. Copyright 9/29/2002 Justin Coslor

Computer Vision Thoughts Classify an object's parts by first cataloging unknown details.
1. Catalog details
2. Catalog association of details
   a. by position
   b. by range of motion
   c. by flexible areas of topography)
3. Catalog repeat patterns.

Gage size and distance by resolution of a known calibration point, or guess. Do so without having to use active sensing such as radar, laser range-finders, etc. Scale images down to the lowest resolution possible while still being able to extract geometric information of a reasonable precision. Write "3D shape-guessing software" that guesses the 3D shape (generalized topography) of objects in a 2D image. It could guess at the dimensions it could not see, and could not change the perspective to any possible side or angle. I know this already exists, but where, and for how much, and is it available anywhere as free open-source software? It could progressively assimilate more complete mappings of objects in view as you feed it more images of the scene or similar scenes. 10/21/2002 Justin Coslor Imaginative new perspectives on famous artworks. Do a painting of Leonardo DaVinci painting the Mona Lisa in the same style and colors as his painting except from a different view point of perspective. Study his self portraits and guess at the unknown details. Do a whole series of paintings of famous artwork scenes but from different perspectives in those same scenes as the originals. All in the same style and colors. Copyright 10/01/2002 Justin Coslor More thoughts on my Thermoelectric Generator Cloth invention 1. Similar to an inverse Peltier junction 2. Could be embedded in hot ceramic resistors to recover thermal energy. It could be used to capture lost heat in electronic circuitry, such as in transistor heat-sinks. It

might need a regulator circuit (which could be embedded on a single
chip) to charge a battery or make use of the electricity directly for
non-critical functions in various circuits. It could be used in cars, on
the under side of the hood and inside of the radiator, and on the
exhaust manifold. it could be used to line hot-air balloons if made thin
enough. It could be used in nuclear power plants It could be wrapped
around radioactive hot rocks for use in space. It could be made out of:
1. metallic powder composites, 2. electroplated wire that can be woven
into a fabric before or after being electroplated. 3. woven dissimilar
metal wire. Inventions: T.E.G. cloth, PDA OCR hand-scanner software
Dremel CNC robotic arm and robotic clamp U CAD/CAM interface software.
Copyright 10/16/2002 Justin Coslor Inventory of revolutionary inventions
that I've invented (but not built) up to this date: 1. Thermo-Electric
Generator Cloth 2. Sine Spiral Graphing for Circular and Complex Motion
3. Conical Orbit Graphing for Satellite Path Visualization and Analysis
4. Dremel CNC Robot (suitcase sized) "Hands Building Hands" robotic
assembly system and haptics interface 5. Library PDA + Hand Scanner
Optical Character Recognition Portable Digitizing System (A software
that could be checked out temporarily from every libary in the world. 6.
New Kind of Cheap Laser-Rangefinder System (use not yet known)...laser
range-finders are normally very expensive. 2/25/2005 Update: I've since
invented a new kind of solid-state crystalline shadow-growth computer
memory device that has no moving parts, that my new kind of
laser-rangefinder would be perfect for accessing and writing the data
to.
6/18/2005 Justin Coslor
Puzzles
    There needs to be more geometric puzzles that people can fiddle with
with their hands while they talk or drink coffee. Some could be games. A
coffee shop could have a tough puzzle or a riddle that they could have
for people to try, where they have to buy a cup of coffee to try it, and
if they solve it they'd get a free cup of coffee. 6/19/2005 Justin
Coslor World medicine Have a worldwide franchise of hydroponic
greenhouses stocked full of medicinal plants. Put one or more in every
town and in each one there'd also be a laboratory and clinic, similar to
how they do in China, but using plants from all over the world. The
clinic would be a front-end for a vast computer medicinal expert system
artificial intelligence, and have a fast full-body scanner in each one
to model their body in 3D for closer inspection. Have a ridiculous
amount of data storage capacity, memory, and computational power, and
have a laser surgery machine and blood analysis equipment, etc. Combine
Western Medicine with Naturopathy, Homeopathy, Accupuncture, Chinese
Herbal Medicine, Native American remedies, Aruveydic medicine, and
South-American Shamantic and Russian (Shamantic and modern) medicine,
and ignore smug know-it-all healer wanna-be's. Medicine goes part of the
way, belief accounts for 40% of healing (according to scientists), and
the rest is basically a gift from God. Do everything possible in the
best possible way and constantly improve all areas. Also have
spiritual/energy healers if you can find good ones or manage to train
them. The fee should be a sliding scale based on a percentage of income,
and have payment plans, which can be partially paid by working in the
greenhouse, lab, or clinic.

                              Book V:
                        Philosophy & Quotes

Some topics I like that I think can really help people and the world:
   I like to study virtue, but I don't necessarily believe in ritual.
It is disturbing when there are rigid thinkers telling people what to do
and think rather than positive possibility thinkers inspiring people to
understand how to be able to appreciate ways of life that are beneficial
and fair for all.
   I like to study logic, particularly epistemology, as it is at the
foundation of everything.
   I like creating multi-purpose adaptable tools, conceptually,
mathematically, and eventually physically, because they add abilities,
perspectives, methods, save time and effort, and in doing so they help
people. That is why I like robotics, intelligent agents on a software
grid, math formulas, mental machinery, and powerful concepts.
   I like psychological enhancement, to get rid of cognitive
dissonance, self-defeating thinking patterns, bad habits, and to train
new skills. Psychology can optimize knowledge bases by gaining new
perspectives that can be used as useful ways to search your memory,
store new memories associatively, and for recombining data from your
memory to develop new and better understanding, as well as enhancing
your perception and awareness by knowing what to look for and by being
aware of areas and topics and things and relations and operations and
systems that might normally be overlooked. Psychology can help increase
intelligence (reasoning ability), hope, motivation, incentive; clarify
and harmonize expectations and emotions, and improve interpersonal
relationships and communication. 7/18/2005 Justin Coslor Applied
Spirituality Applied spirituality is very much like the axiomatic
deductive reasoning system in logic, because each person believes in a
set of spiritual axioms which shape their perceptions and
interpretations, decisions, and judgments, as they progressively shape
and adapt to modifiable and uncontrollable realities in their temporal
collection of experiences, memories, simulations, and navigations; both
physical and perceptual. Spirituality is mostly perceptual navigation
through modes of awareness and conceptual evolution: of concepts that
remain true when perceived of from any level of awareness. If concepts
remain true through different modes of awareness, then the truth is
metaphoric. Many spiritual truths are metaphoric, analogically, across
contexts. Copyright 6/20/2005 Justin Coslor A dream I had
   A few months ago I had this very interesting dream where I was
hiking to a holy place with some friends and when we reached the ancient
sanctuary/shrine we removed several stone/nanotechnology cases, each one
containing a sample of the original strain of some grain and grain-like
foods: corn, wheat, flax, oat, homany, garbanzo beans, etc. They were
each in their own cryogenic case and we couldn't carry all of them and
dropped some on the trail down the mountainside because they were heavy
and bulky. We were carrying them back to base camp. The food samples in
each case were millions of years old, yet still fresh and alive, ready
for planting. After we got them back to camp we got inside some kind of
space craft and traveled through time to a period of civilization where
these plants were wiped out by genetic engineering and plant plagues,
and we planted them there. Note, we didn't manage to get all of them
there because we dropped some down the mountainside and there was great
urgency, but we got most of them to their destination. Then we traveled
back home in the ship, and the pilots took off and this glowing ghostly
time-travelling dragon-like god or alien or something thanked us and it
vanished up into the sky. We returned the remaining cases too before we
got home. I think we had to travel way back in time to get those
samples, then went way into the future, then went back to our original

time. It was a really neat dream. That dragon-being could shape-shift too, and was very powerful, and I remember it being in another one of my dreams which I can't remember right now. Copyright 6/14/2005 Justin Coslor The Dreamworld

The worth of the mind is not its mundane existence in the waking world (which is really the sleeping world -- a world people imprisoned by limitations and thoughtless recursions); the true worth of the mind is in the dream world, where there are unimaginable possibilities manifesting together from parallel universes, past and future, often meaningfully, as if communicated by higher powers for self discovery, experimentation, and exploration of universal truths, with many teachers, friends, lovers, and monsters interacting beyond our control. Dreaming is not about controlling others or characters in the dreams, it's about what we actually decide to do when placed in bizarre situations. There need not be any purpose, but only to experience new forms of perception and interaction. Sometimes it's merely rest, but when our brain is activated fully on during R.E.M. sleep, our mental frequencies, the time-frames of our cognition system, can resonate at higher vibrations so that we can temporarily merge our consciousness with higher dimensional planes where big ideas are anchor points in temporal constructs, and we might share a moment with some advanced beings, or meed some dead relatives who have resonated out of their bodies. There might be portals to any moment or place in existence on higher vibrational time-frames, where we are just a cup of espresso away from Nirvana (or a R.E.M. siesta rather). High activation, Time dilation, Quite a sensation, Deep contemplation. 7/5/2005 Justin Coslor "Violence is not the way to anything but hell." 8/10/2005 Justin Coslor The Philosophy of Nuclear War The philosophy of nuclear war is that %0ïIf I can't have my way during my four year reign of leadership, then I'm going to make the world a radioactive waste dump for the next 50,000 years.%0? Now that's selfish. Copyright 6/23/2005 Justin Coslor Bubble Quote "You're either in a bubble or a cage." 6/20/2005 Justin Coslor The Future

Maybe I should try inventing some new traditions. . . They could be fun yet practical, and totally unenforcible. . .Like having a good stretch every morning and evening, planting a tree every year, and a garden if possible, mailing your old outdated consumer products to some poor 3rd world country family, writing a poem every time something special happens, writing your own book of prayers without crusading them about, saving a percentage of your income, spending time each week in the reference section of the library, not ever being violent under any circumstances, manufacturing some of the things you need and use by hand, etc.

Maybe make some good traditions of your own that'll come in handy in the oncoming ice-age that we're long overdue for. . .global warming has bought us a little bit of extra time before the poles flip and giant icebergs ravage the landscape and dot the oceans south of the Arctic Circle and enormous mountains will rise up in Antarctica and around the tectonic plates, which will scoot around some, setting off volcanic eruptions all around the ring of fire around the world, probably earthquakes too occasionally, as always. Ask your local scientist. Whatever, have a cup of coffee and build yourself a bomb shelter. Good manners were invented for when times get tough. Be polite, honest, humble, and compassionate to everyone. Always. Adapt. -- Justin Coslor Copyright 7/7/2005 Justin Coslor Homo-Sapien Evolution

Maybe mankind evolved into the standing upright posture because females have always generally preferred taller males to shorter ones,

since standing upright makes the male appear taller and thus bigger and more capable of hunting and gathering and protecting the females and young.
Prizes
    When people go from one kind of high or treat to another in life, they keep on going despite any lows or mishaps that happen in between, unless the mishaps convince the person that the whole chase just isn't worth going playing anymore, in which they either commit suicide, change their lifestyle, or get into psychiatric treatment. I believe that suicide is murder, and I refuse to be a murderer under any circumstances. In other situations, such as in the case of the soldier's myth of %Ûİkill or be killed%Û?, I believe that in the long run it's better to die than to take the life of another.
Interconnected Galaxies
    Paper topic/abstract: (I don't know if this theory already exists or how to test it, but I do know that it works on a small scale, which is the whole basis for instantaneous communication devices). Large scale quantum-tunneling between the centers of the galaxies in the universe as part of post-big-bang super-symmetric inverse quantum string theory, but on a very large scale. If space holds a compression, the closer to the center of a galaxy you go the deeper the rabbit hole gets. In other words you can get to any other galaxy by going through the tunnel in the center of the galaxy, which connects to the center of the universe, where you can then just go down one of the tunnels leading in the direction of one of the other galaxies. The next step after that is to figure out how to access the network that links other plurality bubbles (other universes), if such a network on that scale exists within the Monality superstructure (the ordinal of existence) somehow. Star Gate Bubbles form in infinite One, compressions of space, an infinite none. Partitions of One spiral through the none, A cosmic explosion, birthed zillions of suns. Galactic shrapnel, each center a gate through time to the origin of infinite fates. The inverse symmetries tunneled connections innate, from center to Hub to center star gate.
Pulsars
    I think pulsars might be the smaller ends of worm-holes that are rapidly untwisting their tube and spewing energy and matter out the end as they flail around like a runaway fire hose. Worm- holes are spinning black holes that are connected together in the form of a spinning tunnel of compressed time-space. Naturally, if one end is much smaller than the other it will flail around due to the energy rushing through it, and due to the unraveling of the twist in the tube. Pulsars flash multicolored light and are somewhat of a mystery.
Freedom in Sleep Let all of the pain Just wash away With the tides of breath. Submitting to the will of the Universe, I accept what is In life and love -- But hope for what can be. 5/29/2005 Justin Coslor Good Thinking V.S. Flawed Thinking The true crux of the eternal battle between the actions and ideals of good versus the propagation of that which is not, is long-term thinking V.S. short-term thinking. If everyone thought on an extremely long time-frame in their decision making (thus giving up the applicability of the self, i.e. selflessness), past their own lifetime to far future generations ahead, beyond all applicability, their decisions would be geared towards the sustainable support of symbiotic life of all forms, especially friendly highly intelligent life, and well-meaning respect for life forms that are on different paths. Short-term thinking is flawed, and it paves the

way for more flawed thinking. Copyright 2/19/2005 Justin Coslor
Hollywood Quote Hollywood is very dangerous. They literally "program"
people's beliefs, intentions, expectations, and goals. 11/11/2004 Justin
Coslor Do magnets affect time? Time is probably relative to the kinds of
motion that a person or object is doing in physical and Platonic space
because time is a function of motion. I know that when I get inside a
Magnetic Resonance Imaging tube, the powerful superconducting magnets
make it feel like time slows down temporarily, and I can feel the Earth
turn under me. It's a little disorienting. Measuring Progress 11/8/2004
A person's progress is best measured recursively. 11/11/2004 Often over
several lifetimes. 10/28/2004 Justin Coslor Expectations People's
expectations need to be made more pliable and common belief of what is
truly important (such as self-mastery and preventing neglect) need to be
re-evaluated. 10/27/2004 Justin Coslor New Logic Operators Some kinds of
logic use the relations "AND", "OR", "NOT"; but maybe we could make
forms of logic that use the operators "UM", "ER", "UH", "AHA!", "AWE".
Example: 10 UH 10 UH 10 UH, ER, UM, 101010 AHA! 1110 AWE. 10/12/2004
Justin Coslor Motion Motion is the transposition of location from one
configuration to another. Time is a function of motion. 10/28/2004
Justin Coslor Time is only perceptible from a 3rd person perspective on
motion, where the observer's motion is not in parallel to the motion
(transpositions) of the locations (states, set theoretic configurations)
being observed. 1/7/2004 Justin Coslor Notes on the book "Connections:
The Geometric Bridge Between Art & Science" (this book is about Design
Science) Pg. 1. All good design should have: 1. Repetition - some
patterns should repeat continuously. 2. Harmony - parts should fit
together. 3. Variety - it should be non-monotonous (not completely
predictable). ------------------------- 1/10/2005 Notes on the book
Telepathy and the Etheric Vehicle by Alice A. Bailey page 13: 1.
Telepathic communication is
    a. Between soul and mind
    b. Between soul, mind, and brain
This is as far as interior individual development is concerned.
2. When it is found between individuals, telepathic communication is
    a. Between soul and soul.
    b. Between mind and mind.
    c. Between solar plexus and solar plexus, and therefore purely
       emotional.
    d. Between all three of these aspects of energy simultaneously,
       in the case of very advanced people.
3. Telepathic communication is also:
    a. Between a Master and His disciples or disciple.
    b. Between a Master and His group, and a group or groups of
       sensitives and aspirants on the physical plane.
    c. Between subjective and objective groups.
    d. Between the occult Hierarchy and groups of disciples on the
       physical plane. Occult literally means "hidden." Gnosis means
       "hidden knowledge."
    e. Between the Hierarchy and the New Group of world Servers in
order to reach humanity and lift it nearer the goal.
    Page 3: There is a group of Thinkers that falls into the seven main
divisions and is presided over by three great Lives or super-conscious
Entities: the Manu, the Christ, and the Mahachohan. They work primarily
by influencing the minds of the Adepts and the initiates, who then
influence the disciples of the world, and these disciples each in his
own place and on his own responsibility work out their concept of the
plan and seek to give expression to it as far as possible. Page 5: 1.

Telepathy is possible through omnipresence. 2. The interplay of many minds produces a unity of thought which is powerful enough to be recognized by the brain. Page 14: 1. Instinctual telepathy 2. Mental telepathy 3. Intuitional telepathy 1. Initiating agent // communicator // the Knower (Described in books such as the Bhagavad Gita) 2. Recipient // communicant // the Known 3. Medium // communication // the Field of Knowledge.
Copyright 8/13/2005 Justin Coslor Deep Thinking

Each person is like a unique antennae to the knowledge of the universe, and a good adept can interconnect large groups of people spread out over any distance (but local is best), into a gigantic antennae to knowledge in the universe, especially when cosmic thinkers are involved.

There are only about six degrees of separation between everybody on earth; that's a network six node levels deep. Likely one can also interconnect dead people and other forms of life on various planes and remote view a search net around distant galaxies. It seems though that the bottleneck is on methodologies of perception such as language and logics and common ground with other contexts that are based on different sets of axioms than the seeker/observer is aware of. Clarity and perceived/believed utility are also issues. 10/02/2002 Justin Coslor On the outer walls of the main branch of the Carnegie Library of Pittsburgh it says: Carnegie Libary of Pittsburgh - Free to the people The following names carved into the stonework: Homer, Herodotus, Cicero Virgil, Chaucer, Tasso Shakespere, Jonson, Milton Moliere, Pope, Voltaire Goldsmith, Goethe, Scott Irving, Macaulay, Longfellow Emerson, Lowell, Thackeray Dickens, Hawthorne, Tennyson Leonardo, Raphael Michaelangelo, Titian Copernicus, Galileo, Kepler, Newton Buffon, Galvani, Herschel, Laplace Rumford, Fulton, Watt, Stephenson Pythagorus, Aristotle 12/3/2004 Justin Coslor The Soul The Soul is the intelligent Agent personified by the Mind and identified by the body, which holds the record and vectors of intentions and actions and reactions (reactions are caused by expectations) throughout the solitudal and multi-bodied interactions of one's life stages and configurations along growth paths of progression, discovery, exploration, experience, and recursions in finite and universal contexts. NOT COPYRIGHT, FREE FOR UNLIMITED USE 6/5/2005 Justin Coslor Monality and Plurality

In the diagram I drew in 2004 about "One Possible Order Of The Development of Friendly Intelligence", the concept of Monality is the Realm of God, and plurality is the realm of lesser gods (as subsets, or rather partitions of Monality). Monality is infinite oneness; it's all pure energy without space or partitions. It's ultimate interconnectivity, and is the Hub and Vessel of everything. Throw in some partitions or space and you have plurality, which is differentiation and multiplicity. Plurality exists as a network of bubbles inside Monality, each one containing infrastructure that is made of partitions of Monality. God and gods are Intelligences, capable of creating, destroying, harmonizing, and experimenting through any level of plurality through the medium of the Monality of their existence. Probably a lot more too. Location and size are mere variables of ideas and are only comparisons between some perspectives.
Copyright 8/28/2005
Justin Coslor What I Believe

I believe that God exists in omnipresent Monality; partitions of which all things are composed of in this particular bubble in the Monality that our universe and possibly others exist within. Monality is pure energy with no space and no partitions (oneness). Life forms on

this plane and others are configurations of Monality. Life forms are of
innate design coupled with the design of the effects of our decision
making processes throughout our life, and our configurations are also
influenced by the interactions with rest of our environments
(nature/nurture). It takes a bit of epistemological logic and physics
and philosophy to see the reasoning behind all that. Everything I just
write is just an approximation though because all truth is but an
approximation of a deeper truth. Sometimes I'm wrong too. Justin Coslor
Friday, November 12, 2004 Life Rule of Thumb :: Love and Forgiveness
Current mood: thoughtful Life Rule of Thumb This rule of thumb is as
true for life in general as it is for medicine: 1. First, do no harm. 2.
Next, take the route that will do the most good in the long term.
(Always assume there's going to be a long term. Just think cosmic. Look
up into the sky and wonder, and stay positive.) 3. If things aren't
currently working, search for more possibilities, ask for help, and
figure out why. Meditate on it. Deep Prayer is a form of Meditation that
works and can be utilized to help understand things. Science is good
too. Like for carefully perceiving, finding, and manipulating the
building blocks of translatable, augmentable, and adaptable patterns in
contexts. Also, pass on well-intended strategies that work. Also, don't
ever use religion as an excuse to treat people, anyone, or anybody
badly. -- Love and
Forgiveness Typed with additions: 5/1/04 11:10 A.M., and 9/25/2004.
Written by hand: 2/29/2004 This is Copyright 2/29/2004 by me, but you
are free to distribute this text online under the license of The GNU
Public License Agreement (GPL), as long as you include this URL in the
space below, and comply with the GNU Public License Agreement (GPL).
I'll probably publish it in a book at some point, so I reserve the
paperback and hardback book publishing rights for this original
document. 50 percent or more of the proceeds from any booklet, brochure,
magazine article, newspaper article, or any other kind of non-online
printing that comes out of this must go to charity. (Read about the GPL
license on the http://www.gnu.org website for terms of online
redistribution and augmentation.)
----
http://www.myspace.com/index.cfm?fuseaction=user.viewProfile&friendID
=141380 aka: http://myspace.com/dr_octo

Metaphors are geometrical, in a sense, that is to say they follow
mathematical geometries. That is to say, metaphors can be thought of in
terms of geometrical patterns and systems.
-------------------------------- Clairvoyance is the ability to see
patterns within unknown contexts, where the patterns' contexts contain
unknown variables. That is what makes the contexts unknown.
------------------------------ The opposite of love is not hate. The
opposite of love is doubt. Hate is a subset of fear. Fear is a subset of
doubt. Fear comes from a doubt in one's expectations of something, or a
doubt in the position of a game theoretic situation. Anger is a subset
of fear in some cases because it comes from fear of the unknown or fear
of one's own doubt. In other cases anger is a reaction to disrespect,
where one fears that another does not respect them (or fears that
another does not respect themselves or others), and thus does not love
or appreciate them, (love and appreciation are the same thing, but in
varying degrees and ways) because disrespect is rooted in doubt and is
sometimes also linked to fear. One may not have to appreciate or love
something to respect it, but in order to love certain qualities of
something, one must be able to appreciate those qualities (often through

understanding more about them, that's why understanding of good
qualities enhances our ability to recognize and appreciate them in
others (and even learn to find them in ourselves)), though what is good
for one person is not necessarily good or as good for another person).
We all live different versions of the same basic life. Forgiveness is
the permanent action (and decision) of not being angry at someone
(including oneself). In other words, forgiveness is the forgetting of
the painful emotions and judgments brought about by the misdeeds, and
re-framing the memory of the actions themselves into a more
understanding context. A key component of the forgiveness mechanism is
NOT HOLDING A GRUDGE, and adapting ones' own perceptual model to make
true forgiveness possible, and this character-building adaptation is a
form of positive growth, and the adaptation is a virtuous act in itself.
Unforgivingness and unforgiving attitudes create unbounded hostility
that blocks the flow of love, and prevents the healing process from
balancing and proceeding. The intention of forgiveness is to erase
hostilities, and enhance the flow of love. The old saying "Forgive &
Forget" should be "Forgive, Adapt, and Forget". Part of forgiveness is
acceptance for what is, and faith in what can be. When a person adapts,
it is usually much easier to avoid conflict and mishap. Repentance on
the other's part often feels like it is necessary, but repentance takes
time and gradual rebuilding of trust (trust being the foundation of
love), though forgiveness on the victim's part can help motivate the
other person to repent through natural guilt motivation. Forgiving
without negative reaction or provocation, subconsciously tells the
offender that you care about them on a spiritual level regardless of
what they have done to you (that is to say, forgiving them on a very
deep and personal level, which for the moment brings you as close to
them as someone they care dearly about), and that often makes them feel
as bad about hurting you as they would about hurting someone they care
deeply about -as someone who would be capable of understanding them as a
person. At the end of the day, we're all just people. The closeness is
temporal, but the memory of the virtuous act will stick with them and
slowly spiritually guide them towards positive change. These efforts are
progressive and lead towards changing them into a person who is worthy
of such forgiveness. A superficial forgiveness act can be as simple as
shrugging something off instead of placing high priority on your
temporally disrupted sense of trust. The state of one's sense of trust
in a person or group or situation is a major source of emotional
emanations, and events can be looked at simply as information (as the
Stoics taught). Once learned, the skill of forgiveness is so powerful
that it can shine as the most defining element of one's spirit. When
people don't know how to live well, or intensely and deeply why, or
what's going on, then all they can be expected to do is make mistakes.
And as a result, people needlessly suffer and cause unnecessary
suffering, due to their lack of well-intended in-depth questioning. It's
imperative that everyone ask the hard questions, and constantly delve
into critical thinking, so that they can actively seek and find those
profound answers sufficiently. In-depth questioning and intelligent
humble search yields the path of the ultimate quest: to find the ways of
life. That's why enlightenment is such a high priority, because the
enlightened can help to shape the universe lovingly. Love and Logic
(especially wise loving logic), are the greatest of Lore. They are the
primary operators of Truth through the medium of experience. Respect is
acceptance for what is. Repentance is a changing of one's ways to that
which is loving and harmonious, or at least respectful. Love and
forgiveness heals spiritual wounds. Unconditional love requires

unconditional appreciation for some qualities of someone or something,
even if it's just the quality that they appreciate you unconditionally.
I believe that it is everyone's obligation in life to known themselves
and learn about who they are, and as Mahatma Gandhi's nephew once said,
"become the truth that you seek". It is also important to have
acceptance for the parts that you don't love so much, and to try to have
unconditional forgiveness for any and all misdeeds and negative events
of the past. This feat is possible if a person knows themselves well.
Know all the good that you can possibly know, and you'll be well on your
way towards doing good and living well. So the big question is: "Should
forgiveness be dependent on repentance (thus dependent on personal
growth)?" The Prophetic Christ Messiah, Rabbi Jesus of Nazareth, Israel,
commanded (nearly 2000 years ago), that we forgive so that we may be
forgiven by God. Yet despite the obvious disadvantages, many sects of
the Jewish and Islamic faiths have stuck with the "eye for an eye, tooth
for a tooth" philosophy for thousands of years. Though too many
so-called "Christians" have done no better in wartime as well as on a
day-today basis. So many people unfortunately cling to fading allusions
of purity, righteousness, and belief in the rite to avenge (the rite of
revenge), as an excuse to treat each other badly (including their own
people) and murder each other in "wars". I don't care how people try to
justify it, or what kind of merit badges they hand out; killing people
is murder, any way you look at it, and in every situation, killing
people is murder. It is so painfully obvious that the only true
sanctuary and justice is through selfless virtue, which is only
attainable on an individual level, and discovering that paradise is
within oneself, not in their surroundings, but in the nature of their
connection to the universe itself. The world is long overdue for an
update by advanced beings, since it seems to be currently controlled by
the manipulative misinforming public media, the individual egos of
various predatory authority figures, and a minority of rich nonelect.
Let's work together to make the world a better place, and to lay stable
foundations for the sustainability of future generations on Earth.

---------- Violence is not the way, and two wrongs do not make a right.
Oh, btw, most of the Gospels written about Jesus were either burned or
rewritten by the Cathars, er, I mean the Catholic Church...So don't
assume that you know what true Christianity is all about unless you're a
psychic metaphysician or something. Regardless of whether or not you
feel the need for a messiah, or believe in the concept of one, there's a
lot of useful wisdom in scripture from many religions and meditations,
and that's what's most important. Nobody is perfect, since life is an
interconnected cyclic progression; and nobody is 100 percent correct
about everything, since all perspectives are but an approximation of the
whole Truth; but the gems shine through, and can be learned. There have
been prophets living on the Earth at all times in human history, whether
or not people notice them, and regardless of which path to God the
people and the prophets themselves choose to take or acknowledge. Nobody
is inherently better than anybody else under God, because a person can
only truly be compared to themselves, and a person's progress is best
measured recursively, often over several lifetimes. We must all be
humble. Virtue is a gift of intelligent choice that one decides to give
to themselves. It cannot be bought, it cannot be sold, and it certainly
cannot be handed down, but can merely be laid out in part by example and
through education of good wisdom, as an option to consider for oneself.
Some ways just work better than others, and of the ways that work, some
ways work better than other ways for certain people. People eventually

figure out the ways that support life (hopefully), often with a little help from a friend. The gist of the Creation V.S. Evolution debate to me is that creation implies genetic engineering, whereas evolution implies natural selection over long periods of time. Either way, it's survival of the fittest, but genetic engineering is largely based on the genetic expression of traits that arose through natural selection, that have then been pieced together to make a hybrid life-form. I believe that both occurred in our development. People often are too concerned with their physical forms, as opposed to their spiritual progress, and this debate is a perfect example. Reincarnation does occur until the end-time, however nobody knows when that may be, or even whether or not they will be granted a chance to reincarnate.
-- A wise man once wrote "There are three things you need to be happy in life: Something to do, Someone to love, and Something to look forward to." Justin Coslor 04/24/2005 More thoughts on the philosophy of love... "Doubt not, and your love will be unconditional." Excerpts from Justin's Journal 4/8/2004 In any complex situation, I think this is a good rule to stick to: Prepare for the worst, Hope for the best, Allow plenty of room for the unexpected, and Know what to do next. 5/5/2004 Almost any given moment can be a decision point, and at every waking moment we are subconsciously and/or consciously either acting out old intentions, or enacting new intentions. It is very important to be mindful of our intentions in stressful situations, and not to allow our subconscious (or conscious) intentions to in any way hinder or suppress the free will of others. It is also important to nurture good intent in ourselves and others, and to consciously guide the focus back into the range of good intent whenever it gets very far off track. Positive thinking goes a long way, but it should always be coupled with good intent towards all parties in order to solve problems in the long run. Positive thinking + good intent = answers.
      -Justin Coslor 8/7/2005 Justin Coslor Appreciation We need to try to be worthy of all of the effort that God went to to create us and to allow us to exist in His universe. The universe is an unfathomably gigantic and mostly empty space (on this vibrational plane of time/motion), full of ridiculously powerful forces and chaos, and the best that we can hope for is the sustainable evolution of symbiotic life, and to make friends along the way. 8/8/2005 Eventually everyone will be as smart as the geniuses of today, and much smarter as we evolve together in many ways. 8/8/2005 Humans have only been around for a minuscule fraction of the time-line of life on Earth, and as such we're still an unproven and rather experimental form of life, but we have a lot of potential and a long way to go. 4/30/2005 Justin Coslor Paper topic: Ways to heighten interest and ways of inspiring motivation. --> Re-map expectations Dangle a carrot over core knowledge bases Be friendly, helpful, and set a good example. Support eternal questioning, but not eternal doubting. Inquiry needs to be free of judgments and rigidity. Perspective is retrospective. Truth is found as patterns in contexts. Motivation is a balance of hope and incentive. Keep values in mind and alive; meaning value all seekers of truth, the journey, the accomplishments and milestones, and the lessons learned preemptively and from mistakes and hardship of chance. Add more later. . .write a paper. 5/1/2005 --> The purpose of life is to survive and evolve, but the higher purpose of life is to find and share appreciation. To appreciate and to be appreciated, to find and share insight: that is the basis of value. 1-16-2005 Justin Coslor Here's one of my philosophies: "Motivation is dependent on inspiration, hope of success, and incentive

to do whatever there is to be done." 11-24-2003 Justin Coslor. Information Theory Quote: Information is a symphony of symbolism and symmetry. Perls of wisdom strung in a ring, tossed in the sky, away they fly. Copyright Justin Coslor 1-19-2005 Resume: Justin M. Coslor Post Office Box 367 Mount Vernon, Washington State 1 (360) 856-1776 JustinCoslor@gmail.com http://frdcsa.org/~justin Education: - Sedro-Woolley High School - Graduated 1998, GPA 3.89, skipped 1 year. - Skagit Valley Community College - Electronics Fundamentals - 1995 - Carnegie Mellon University - Completed about one semester, in 1997-1998. (I had some medical obstacles while at CMU that held me back.) CMU courses completed: English, Math in Context (Philosophy Dept. freshman survey course), introductory Statistics, introductory Psychology, Calculus, Computer Skills Workshop. - South Seattle Community College - Technical Writing, TIG Welding - 1999 Work Experience: - K-Mart - Consumer Electronics Dept. Cashier - 1997 - CMU Alumni House - Telephone Fund-raiser (Work-Study Job) - 1998 - CMU Dept. of Computer Science - Troubleshooting a robotic cassette player manufacturing system (Work-Study Job) - 1998 - Kelly Temporary Services - Temp Jobs in Seattle - 1999 - CMU Housing Dept. - Desk Attendant (Work-Study Job) - 1999 - CMU Dept. of Computer Science - Volunteer - Assisted in mechanical fabrication and design of a pre-prototype mock-up of a robotic ice- drilling lunar rover - 2000 - Manpower Temporary Services - Temp Jobs in Seattle - 2000 - Jewish Community Center - Cashier - Cafe J Snack Shop - 2003 - The Home Outlet Hardware Store - Customer Service, Sales Cashier, Key-making, and Computer Repairman - 2003-2004 Skills: I have primarily computer skills, writing skills, and shop skills. My computer experience includes some Mac Skills, strong Microsoft Windows Skills, some Linux Skills, and some HTML. I know how to install hardware and software, and how to update device drivers from Online sources. I'm excellent at corresponding remotely via email. I learn new software applications very quickly. I have excellent Online price comparison shopping skills, and excellent Online research skills. I'm quite organized and analytical, and often inspirational. I'm very good at preparing and giving presentations: ask me about this. Possibility thinking, conceptualizing, writing, and reasoning are my strong suits, and I consider those to be my most valued skills. I tend to get along very well with everybody, but especially with creative people and computer programmers. Objective: Part time low stress work where could do some writing and reasoning. and or design. Typing. Creative composition. Computing Skills: Programming: basic HTML, basic C/C++ Platforms: DOS (5,6.22), Windows (3.1, 95, NT, 98SE/Me, 2000/XP), Linux (Debian 3.0, Knoppix 3.2), Mac (<= 8), PalmOS 5.21 Applications, as elicited through an interview: - Word processing: Word, Emacs, Abiword, OpenOffice, Notepad, Wordpad, pico - News/Email: Outlook Express, Netscape Communicator, Eudora, Opera, Evolution, Konquerer - Project Management: Planner, Stickynotes - IRC: mIRC - BBS: MajorBBS, RenegadeBBS - IM: Trillian, Yahoo Messenger, MSN IM, AIM, Tik, Zephyr, ntalk, ytalk - File Transfer: WsFTP, Hotline, NcFTP, FTP, Synaptic Package Manager, apt-get - Terminal Client: telnet, finger, ping, man, cd, mv, mkdir, rmdir, ls, chmod, pwd, locate, wildcards, irc, pico, emacs (still learning), <tab> for auto-completion of paths. - System Administration: DiskDefrag, Norton SpeedDisk, Norton Antivirus, ZoneAlarm Firewall - MS: Word, Powerpoint, Excel, Access, Frontpage - Adobe: Pagemaker, Photoshop, Acrobat Reader - WWW Browsers: Lynx, Mozilla, Netscape, IE, Opera - PDA Device: Palm Zire 71 (PalmOS 5.21) - General: Software/Hardware/Driver installation/upgrades, Online research, price comparison, setup internet connections. - Typing: Touch,

WPM: >45wpm
Mon 22 Oct 2007 11:32:42 PM EDT http://frdcsa.org/~justin
    Universally Free Everywhere Forever for Friendly Intelligence uses
only that are compatible with this essay. Please: this is never ever to
be used whatsoever for treating anyone or anything badly. I sometimes believe
I can and will evolve my ethics to the point where no one is able to upset
me without anyone treating me badly. I think the key is in never
treating anyone badly whatsoever and in always treating everyone well
and being Stoic to negativity and ignorance and harm against me by
treating such abuse and short-term flawed thinking merely as information
which can be upgraded via education into positive long-term thinking and
well-meaning behavior that has positive results for everyone and no
negative repercussions for anyone and that is fair and honest and kind
and helpful and peaceful and non-harmful and humble and compassionate
and egalitarian and friendly to everyone and everything, and logical and
unselfish in the long term, the short term, and all of the moments in
between in all imaginable contexts, including other peoples. Also I
believe that it is essential to try to see the best in everyone and in
everything and to try to be at my best so that there is a better chance
of a smooth transition and of bringing out the best in everyone and of
bringing about harmony, love, truth, logic, and great positive
possibilities and realities.
Mon 05 Nov 2007 8:27 PM
http://frdcsa.org/~justin/writing3
ONE GOD = HAVE NO OTHER GOD
NO IDOLATRY = WORSHIP GOD NOT FEAR
NO BLASPHEME = SWEAR NOT
HONOR SABBATH = A DAY OF REST TO REMEMBER
HONOR PARENTS = BE THANKFUL
NO KILL = DO NO MORTAL HARM
NO ADULTERY = HONOR MARRIAGE
NO STEAL = GIVE FREELY
NO LIE = BE HONEST
NO COVET = HAVE POSITIVE BELIEF AND FORGIVE (covet = jealousy = envy)
Exodus 20:3-17
1. ONE no law until an election
2. TWO no law of religion
3. THREE free exercise
4. FOUR free speech
5. FIVE free press
6. SIX free people
7. SEVEN free petition
The separation of church and state is necessary.
ABCDEFGHIJKLMNOPQRSTUVWXYZ
abcdefghijklmnopqrstuvwxyz
123456789
10 11 12 13 14 15 16 17 18 19
20 21 22 23 24 25 26 27 28 29
30 31
1 2 3 5 7 11 13 17 19 23 29 31
1 2 3 4 5 6 7 8 9 10 11 12
SUSPICION IS THE DOWNFALL OF MANY
WITHOUT PRIVACY THERE IS NO FREEDOM
WITHOUT FREEDOM THERE IS NO LIBERTY
WITHOUT LIBERTY THERE ARE NO TOOLS
WITHOUT TOOLS THERE IS NO LIFE
EVEN OUR SPIRITS AND MINDS AND BODIES ARE TOOLS

ALL LIFE IS AND MAKES AND USES TOOLS
There is Wisdom in many places
from many times, many spaces.
All the world is just one world
no less important than another.
Wisdom comes from God and knowledge is translated wisdom.
Ethics is knowledge that should be tested shared and taught;
never construed for abuse and never violently fought.
Negative assumptions should be challenged at heart
by long-term positive perspectives to redo their start.
Perspective is introspective and retrospective,
an inspirational directive.
A context is a continuum of perspective,
as a network of patterns.
A pattern is a network of adjectives,
as a network of symmetry and synchronicity.
Information is a symphony of symbolism and symmetry.
Sometimes ideas come before their understanding.
Ideas that are understood form a continuum of perspective.
Positivity is harmony with peace at its core,
merciful and compassionate and honest and humble and more.
There is always more as that is what ideas are for.
Mistakes come from short term thinking such as selfishness and harm.
To be supportive is to be trusting, appreciative, hopeful, and warm.
It is essential to always be honest and not rude.
If these ideas are forgotten this life may seem crude.
To do unto others as you would have others do unto you
is to treat everyone well so that there can be sanctuary for all.
Each home is important and is as important as every other.
Each person is important and is as important as every other.
Diversity is essential and is like a university.
Together we learn to avoid temptations such as anger and lust and greed.
Even before we do, the Universe knows exactly what we need.
Each of us is an origin, a destination, and a seed of hope.
http://frdcsa.org/~justin/writing3
Please remember to try not treat anyone badly.

www.ingramcontent.com/pod-product-compliance
Lightning Source LLC
Chambersburg PA
CBHW022119280326

41933CB00007B/464